Golden Album Quilt

20 PATCHWORK PATTERNS

JINNY BEYER

Breckling Press

Library of Congress Cataloging-in-Publication Data

Beyer, Jinny.

  Golden album quilt : 20 patchwork patterns / Jinny Beyer.

     p. cm.

  Includes bibliographical references.

  ISBN 978-1-933308-28-9

  1. Patchwork--Patterns. 2. Quilting--Patterns. 3. Patchwork quilts. I.

Title.

  TT835.B4294 2010

  746.46'041--dc22

                      2010038190

This book was set in ITC Galliard and Bickham Script

Editorial and production direction by Anne Knudsen

Interior design by Maria Mann·

Published by Breckling Press

283 Michigan Ave., Elmhurst IL 60126 USA

Printed and bound in China

International Standard Book Number: 978-1-933308-28-9

Acknowledgments

This pattern book came about because I received so many emails from people wanting to know if there was a pattern for the quilt on the cover of *The Quilter's Album of Patchwork Patterns*. The image on the cover of that book was not a quilt, but a collage of block images. After receiving so many inquiries, I decided to create a quilt based on many of the blocks on the cover.

First, I wish to thank all of the people who emailed me to ask for a quilt. I also want to thank Carole Nicholas who sewed many of the blocks in the quilt sample, Elaine Kelly, who helped with the patterns, and the members of the monthly Jinny Beyer Club at my shop who tested the patterns. I also want to thank my publisher, Anne Knudsen, who always, does such a superb job of producing my books, and designer Maria Mann for her excellent layout.

Golden Album Quilt, Jinny Beyer, 2010. 62" x 70"

Contents

T his collection of 20 patchwork patterns was created in response to requests from readers of my encyclopedia for quilters, *The Quilter's Album of Patchwork Patterns*. When I designed the cover of that book, I wanted a collage of quilt blocks that were compatible with each other and that also showed a sampling of what was inside the encyclopedia. Working with digital files, I played around with a selection of quilt blocks until I was satisfied with the effect.

Once the book was published I started to receive emails from quilters who wanted to know if there was a pattern for the quilt on the cover of the book. Since the design had been created digitally, there really was no actual quilt. Still, I decided that the arrangement of blocks would make an interesting design, so I adapted it into a quilt measuring 62" x 70". The patterns and instructions for making it are presented here.

You can use the patterns several ways. You can, of course, make the quilt exactly as it is shown on the cover of this book. You can also repeat a single block or alternating blocks to make an entire quilt with an overall mosaic design. More challenging, you can also play around with the arrangement and sizes of the blocks to create an entirely new quilt of your own. The tools are all here, but the choice is yours.

The Quilt Design

The quilt is made up of three different sized blocks ($6\frac{3}{8}$", $10\frac{1}{8}$" and $13\frac{7}{8}$"), set into four modules that contain five blocks each. The blocks and modules are separated by sashing strips. Two of the modules are reversed as shown here. Note that the two modules on the right are rotated 180 degrees from the two on the left.

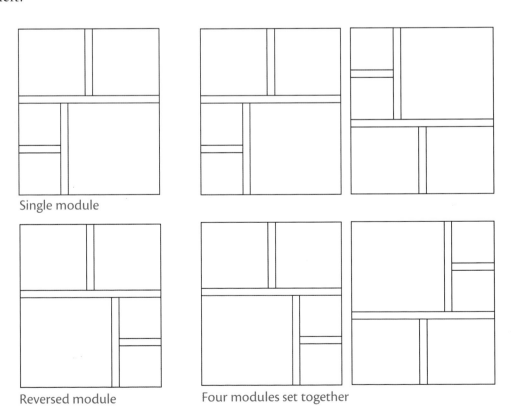

Single module

Reversed module   Four modules set together

BLOCK SIZES

The size of the blocks is determined by the width of the strip used for sashing. **For this quilt design, the sashing strips have a finished width of 1⅛". In order to use the patterns in this book the fabric you select for the sashing must allow for that finished width.** This means that, once seam allowance is added in, the sashing must be 1⅝" wide. If you choose a sashing fabric that is narrower or wider, you will need to redraft the blocks and make your own patterns, so that everything fits together as it should. (For help on redrafting blocks, refer to my encyclopedia, *The Quilter's Album of Patchwork Patterns.*)

If you decide to use a finished sashing width wider or narrower than 1⅛", here is how to determine the size of blocks you need.

1. Begin with the smallest block. This can be any finished size you want. Put two squares of that size side by side, separated by the width of the sashing. If you begin with a 6" block (finished) and your sashing is 1" wide (finished), then those three sewn together will measure 13".

2. The largest block in the quilt design measures the size of two of the smallest blocks, plus the width of the sashing strip. Continuing the example from Step 1, the finished size of the largest block must be 13". The largest block is sewn to the two smaller ones and is connected by a strip of the sashing, so now that unit is 13" plus 1" plus 6", for a total of 20".

3. The 20" unit is sewn onto the two remaining (medium sized) blocks which are also separated by a strip of sashing. Subtract the 1" sashing strip and divide the resulting 19" in two. The medium-sized blocks must be a finished size of 9½".

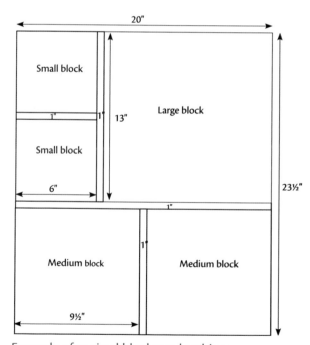

Example of re-sized blocks and sashing

Fabric

Thirteen different fabrics are used in the *Golden Album Quilt*. These fabrics, are shown in the Fabric Chart (on page 3). The focal point of the quilt is the border print fabric. It is used in all of the blocks. If you plan on creating the quilt as it is shown on the cover, you will need to select a border print fabric that contains a narrow stripe that is 1⅛" wide. Select your border print fabric, then coordinate the rest of the fabrics with it.

Golden Album Quilt: Fabric Chart

Fabric 1
5 ½ yds — All blocks

Fabric 2
¼ yd — 6, 7, 15

Fabric 3
½ yd — 3, 9, 10, 11, 16

Fabric 4
½ yd — 8, 12, 17, 19, 20

Fabric 5
¼ yd — 13, 14

Fabric 6
¼ yd — 1, 4, 18

Fabric 7
¼ yd — 7, 10, 13, 18

Fabric 8
⅝ yd — 2, 6, 8, 11, 15, 17, 19

Fabric 9
⅛ yd — 11, 16, 20

Fabric 10
¼ yd — 2, 4, 9, 11, 12, 15

Fabric 11
¼ yd — 2, 5, 17, 20

Fabric 12
1 ¾ yd — 1, 5, 6, 16, 19

Fabric 13
⅝ yd or enough for 20 mirror-image motifs — 18, 19

Fabric 14
¾ yd — Binding

Fabric 15
4¾ yd — Backing

Finished quilt size: 62" x 70"
Block sizes: 6⅜", 10⅛", 13⅞"
First border: 1¾" wide
Second border: 2¼" wide
Third border: 5" wide

Once you have selected your border print, other fabrics needed include:

- Three gold fabrics
- Four red fabrics
- Five different background fabrics

The variety of background fabrics gives textural interest to the quilt. If you prefer to use all one background, combine the yardage amounts shown on the fabric chart.

For Fabric 13, one of the reds used in two of the blocks, try to find a fabric that has mirror-imaged motifs. By centering the mirror-imaged motif in the middle of the template, secondary patterns appear. If you cannot find a print with mirrored motifs, a second coordinating border print fabric would also work for cutting mirrored motifs. You will need 20 mirrored motifs—eight identical ones for the points of the stars in *Silver Star* and *White Nights*. *White Nights* also has four mirrored motifs in the corners of the block. The number of mirrored motifs and the repeat of the design will dictate how much yardage to purchase.

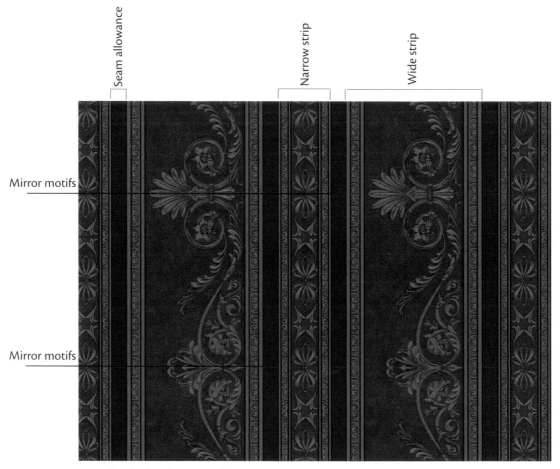

Sample of a border print fabric

A NOTE ABOUT GRAIN

When I add borders to a quilt, I prefer all fabrics to be cut on the *straight* grain of the fabric as opposed to the *cross* grain. This helps to keep the borders from ruffling. They stay nice and straight and they can be cut all in one piece, without seams. Therefore, the yardage for borders has been calculated to allow the long strips for the middle border to be cut all in one piece. If you prefer to purchase less fabric, you can buy 1 yard of fabric instead of 1¾ yards. You will have to cut the fabric strips for the middle border across the width of the fabric and there will be a seam on each of these sides.

Using Border Print Fabrics

Border prints are fabrics made up of repeat stripes with decorative designs. These types of fabrics are a "focus print" in each of my fabric collections. In my designs there are two different stripes—one narrow and one wider—and each is repeated at least four times across the width of the fabric. There are mirrored motifs in the stripes at the repeating points. Each of the stripes is separated by at least ½" so the stripes can be cut apart while still allowing a standard ¼" seam allowance on each one.

Narrow and wide stripes in border print fabric

A border print fabric is one of the main elements in *Golden Album Quilt*. The stripes not only frame the quilt and the blocks, but are also used extensively within the individual blocks. Half of the blocks have triangles cut from the border print, eight of them have rectangles where strips of the border print have been used, two have octagons made up of eight smaller triangles, and one of them has squares made up of four triangles.

In all cases, these border print pieces should be cut with a mirror image motif centered in the middle of the shape and all pieces in any given block should be cut in an identical manner. A mirror line marked on the template acts as a guide for centering these motifs.

Border Prints Used in Shapes

One aspect of working with border prints that I particularly like is the fact that the various shapes can be outlined using a small stripe from the print. Therefore, when cutting out the pieces, I like to place the template on the fabric so that the portion of the template that will form the *outside* of the shape will fall along one of the straight-line edges of the border print. I make sure that this line falls just within the sewing line so that it will still be visible when all the pieces of the shape are sewn together. This techniques is described on the next page.

Fabrics with mirror image designs

Border Print Squares

Many patchwork blocks have squares as part of the design, where the square is further divided into four triangles. These blocks present a perfect opportunity to use a border print. *Prosperity Block* (see page 42) is one such block, as it has areas of the design where four identical triangles come together to form squares. These triangles present a perfect opportunity to use a border print. To make a border print square, follow these steps.

Prosperity Block

1. Using semi-transparent template material, make a template from one of the triangles that includes a ¼" seam allowance around all sides. (It is easy to create a triangle template in any size you need by cutting a square diagonally in four).

2. Draw a line down through the middle of the template. This line will be used as a guide for centering the motifs of the fabric. To do this, line one of the short sides of a right angle, 45-degree triangle along the *long* edge of the triangle template and bring the other short edge to the right angle on the template. Draw the line.

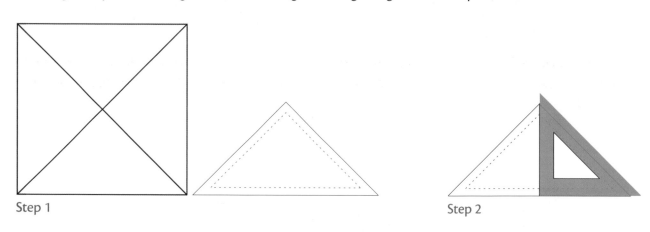

Step 1

Step 2

3. Using the line marked in step 2 as a guide, center the template on one of the mirror-image motifs in the border-print fabric, making sure that a line from the border print falls just inside the sewing line on the long side of the triangle template. This ensures that you will have a nice line or frame around the outside of the finished square. With the template in place on the fabric, trace some portion of the design directly onto the template. As you move the template to cut the other pieces, this mark can be used as a guide for lining up the template in the same exact place as the first triangle. Carefully draw around the template to mark the fabric and cut the piece out. Then cut three more triangles identical to the first one.

Step 3

4. Sew the four triangles together, carefully matching the design on the border print at the edges. If you want to see what the finished shape will look like before actually cutting into the fabric, place the template onto the fabric in the place where you think you want to cut. Then carefully place two hinged square mirrors onto the seam allowance of the template. Place these mirrors on the two sides that will be sewn to create the shape. Gently remove the template and the image in the mirror will show you how the finished piece will look once it is sewn together.

Step 4

It is amazing how many different squares you can cut from the same border strip by simply placing the template on a slightly different portion of the fabric. The squares shown here illustrate just a few possibilities from the border print shown in step 3.

Variety of patterns created from the same border print fabric

Border Print Octagons

Many patchwork designs have a perfectly symmetrical octagon in the center of the block. Sometimes this is one entire octagon and sometimes it has been broken down into eight triangles. If there is a plain octagon, I often break it down into the triangles so that I can incorporate a border print, using a technique similar to the one I use for border print squares. Follow the same process as the square, but this time cut eight identical triangles from the border print. Just as with the triangle template for creating a square, mark a line down the center of the template and then center that line on a mirror-imaged portion of the fabric. Draw a portion of the design on the template to use as a guide for cutting the remaining triangles. Make sure that all triangles are cut exactly the same.

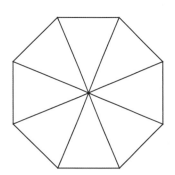  

Make a border print octagon

Mirrored fabrics as well as border prints can create kaleidoscopic effects in quilts. Mirrored fabrics create particularly interesting effects in star, sunflower, and mariner's compass type patterns. Fabric 13 used in *Golden Album Quilt* has mirror-imaged motifs and was used in *White Nights* and *Silver Star*. The process is exactly the same as working with border-print fabrics. Center the template to be used over a mirror-imaged portion of the fabric. Mark part of the design onto the template so that the remaining pieces can be cut exactly the same. See the difference in these two blocks, when the mirrored fabric is replaced with a non-mirrored one.

Mirrored fabric in *White Nights*

Using Templates

One of the most important parts of making a quilt is to ensure that the fabric pieces are cut with accuracy. Since the blocks that make up this quilt are an odd size, it would be difficult to rotary cut strips and squares for creating the pieces. Therefore templates for each piece in each pattern are included in a section at the back of the book (see pages 60 to 80).

The pattern pieces have two lines around the edges. The solid line is the cutting line and the dashed line is the sewing line. These two lines are ¼" apart, which is the seam allowance. If you have drafted the patterns in a different size, you will have to add the ¼" seam allowance around all sides of all pieces.

Several of the blocks have small circles on some of the templates at some of the angles where the seam allowances touch. These circles indicate "pivot points", needed when one piece has to be set into two other pieces. On these pieces, the stitching must stop at these circles, not extend into the seam allowance.

Some of the templates have a line down the middle called a *mirror line*. That line is used for the pieces cut from the border print fabric and the other fabric with mirrored motifs.

Arrows on the templates indicate grain line. To eliminate distortion of the blocks, it is best to have the cross or straight grain of the fabrics along the outside edges of the block. This cannot always happen when cutting from a border print fabric. When cutting the pieces, place this arrow on the cross or straight grain of the fabric. Note that some pattern pieces are used for cutting two different fabrics and in some cases there are two arrows. A note on the template indicates which fabric the different arrows refer to.

My favorite template material is rigid, semi-transparent plastic (no grid lines). It comes in sheets that are approximately 11" x 17".

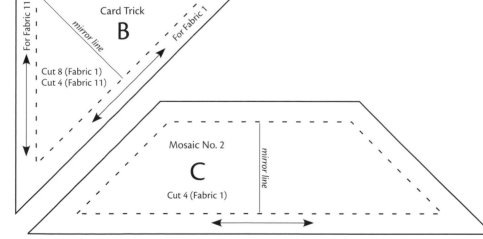

Sample templates showing mirror line, pivot points, and other markings.

1. Place the template plastic directly over the pattern in the book or your drafted design and trace each piece onto the plastic. I like to place a short ruler or my Jinny Beyer Perfect Piecer (see page 12) along the line, and mark along the edge of the ruler with a fine-lined permanent marking pen.

2. Trace any identification marks or grain lines and both the cutting and sewing lines. Use a permanent marker to record all identification letters and lines that appear on each pattern piece, as well as the size and name of the block and the number of pieces needed. If you have drafted your own pattern, use the Jinny Beyer Perfect Piecer or a ruler with ¼" lines marked to add an exact seam allowance around all sides of each piece. Place the Perfect Piecer along the "sewing" line, with ¼" extending beyond that line. Mark along the edge of the ruler. This will allow for the ¼" seam allowance.

3. Using a sharp pair of scissors, cut around the template piece on the solid cutting line. Do not use your good fabric scissors for cutting templates as the plastic causes them to blunt quickly. Alternately, place a ruler along the cutting line and cut using a rotary cutter.

4. Double check your templates against the pattern for accuracy.

Step 2

Cutting the Pieces for the Quilt

RESERVING FABRIC FOR THE BORDERS
Before cutting any of the pieces for the blocks, reserve the fabrics that will be needed for the sashing and borders of the quilt. These pieces will be cut from Fabric 1 (the border print) and Fabric 12 (the middle border). Whatever is left over from these pieces will be used in the blocks.

From Fabric 1
Sashing: Reserve 10½ yards by 1⅝" of a narrow border stripe. The border stripe itself should be 1⅛", with ¼" on either side for seam allowance.

*Border 1: Reserve two 54" and four 36" strips of border stripe (finished size of stripe is 1¾" with seam allowance on either side for a total width of 2 ¼").

*Border 3: Reserve two 81" and four 54" strips of 5 ½" wide border stripe.

* *Note*: Depending on the border print that you select, these narrow and wide stripes for the borders of the quilt may not be the widths described above. This will not matter. It is the *length* of the strips that is important. The only border stripe width that is crucial is the one used for the sashing between the blocks, because that will determine the size of the blocks used in the quilt. The blocks for *Golden Album Quilt* have been sized based on a finished sashing width of 1⅛".

From Fabric 2
Border 2: Reserve four 63" strips of 2¾" border stripe.

CUTTING THE FABRICS FOR THE BLOCKS
Each pattern has a Template Guide and a Fabric Guide. Each of the pattern pieces is indicated by a letter of the alphabet on the Template Guide. The numbers on the Fabric Guide indicate which fabrics are used in the block (see Fabric Chart on page 3).

1 ⅝" sashing strip including seam allowance

1 ⅛" sashing strip: finished size

Border 3: 5½" strip of border stripe including seam allowance

Border 1: 2¼" strip including seam allowance

Border 1: 1¾" strip, finished size

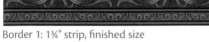

Border 3: 5" strip of border print, finished size

Reserve fabric for borders

MARKING THE PATTERN ONTO THE FABRIC

In order to cut out the pattern pieces you will need to mark the shape of each piece onto the fabric. Clover Company makes a triangular shaped tailor's chalk that comes in four colors—red, blue, yellow and white. This chalk is my favorite tool for marking around templates. The red or blue chalk shows up well on light colored fabric and the white or yellow shows up well on dark colored fabric. The chalk has a sharp edge on all three sides. When this edge begins to dull, it can easily be sharpened with an emery board or a piece of sand paper. I have also used a knife or pair of paper cutting scissors to gently scrape the chalk into a sharp edge again.

CUTTING THE PIECES

The pattern templates indicate how many pieces to cut of each fabric. I often cut two pieces at a time. However, *Golden Album Quilt* was designed specifically to show a variety of ways that a border print could be used in patchwork blocks. Every block uses the border print in some way, and these pieces must be cut with care. Since you will be centering the template on specific portions of the design, each one of these border print pieces must be cut individually. (See pages 5 to 8 on working with border prints.)

When cutting the pieces, orient the template so that the arrow falls on the cross or straight grain of the fabric.

Jinny Beyer Perfect Piecer

The Jinny Beyer Perfect Piecer, used by both machine and hand sewers, is a tiara shaped tool I designed primarily for marking seam allowances and the points where seam allowances cross to help sewers know where to start and stop stitching. It includes all the common angles used in patchwork. Holes are pre-punched in this master template at the precise points where the seam allowances will cross and along the quarter inch seam allowance line. Even though the original idea was for the Perfect Piecer to be an aid in marking seam allowances, it can be used for so much more and it is my constant companion when sewing and drafting. I also use it as a ruler, as a straight edge, as a small right triangle, and for mitering borders that are less than 3" wide.

Marking Seam Allowances

If your templates have an exact quarter inch added and you have cut accurately, then you only need to mark the seam allowance on the piece of fabric that will be *on top* when you stitch. Line up the cut edges and as long as the seam allowance is correctly marked on the top piece, there is no need for a line on the back piece.

There are two ways to use the Perfect Piecer for marking seam allowances. The first is to lay the dotted seam line just outside the edge of the cut shape. Then, using a sharp tailor's chalk or mechanical chalk pencil, draw a line along the edge of the piecer.

The second way to mark a seam allowance is to align the edge of the Perfect Piecer along the edge of the cut shape. Then, using a mechanical chalk pencil or a hard lead mechanical pencil, mark dots on the shape through the holes that run along the quarter-inch mark on the Perfect Piecer.

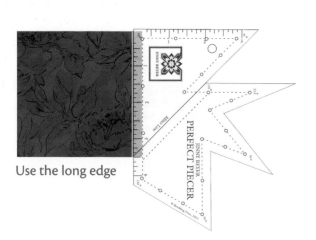

Use the long edge

Use pencil to mark dots through holes

When sewing curves, it is crucial that the seam allowance is exact. Use a series of dots for the sewing line and then sew dot to dot. Place the right angle (90 degree) corner of the Perfect Piecer on the curved shape, as shown, with the edge of the piecer at the edge of the fabric. Mark a dot through the hole at the 90 degree mark. Still keeping the edge of the Perfect Piecer at the edge of the fabric, move by increments around the curve and make a series of dots.

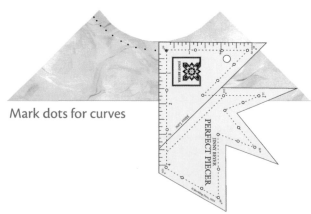

Mark dots for curves

Marking Angles and Points

Often in patchwork it is necessary to have set-in seams. For these seams, you must begin and end stitching at the places where the seam allowances cross. The most common angles in the shapes used for patchwork designs are 22.5 degrees, 30 degrees, 45 degrees, 60 degrees, 90 degrees, 120 degrees and 135 degrees. All these angles are marked on the Perfect Piecer. Each of the angles has a hole at the exact spot where the seam allowances meet.

Find the angle on the Perfect Piecer that corresponds with the angle on the fabric. Place the tip of a mechanical chalk pencil through the hole and mark a dot on the fabric. Most of the angles are readily apparent because they are on the outside edges of the Perfect Piecer.

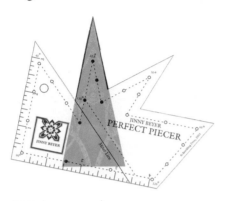

22.5 degree angle

45 degree angle

The 135 degree angle is different, and is at first confusing. This angle runs along the miter line marked on the Perfect Piecer, and then angles up to the 22.5 degree dot. The 135 degree angle is an often used angle since it is one of the angles in a 45 degree diamond. It is also the angle that needs a dot on the mitered edges of a border print.

To mark the 135 degree angle, place the miter line along the left side of the angle on the fabric and then move the Perfect Piecer until the edge that goes to the 22.5 degree angle falls along the right side edge of the fabric. The two diagrams here show this angle. The first shows the angle on a 45 degree diamond and the second shows the angle on a mitered border fabric.

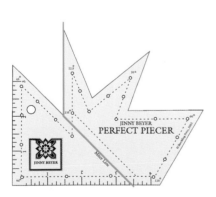

135 degree angle marked in yellow

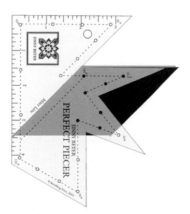

135 degree angle on a
45 degree diamond

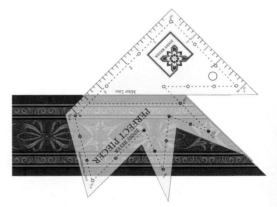

135 degree angle on a mitered border

Right Triangles

The Perfect Piecer can be used as a right triangle, whether drafting patterns, cutting miters for borders or marking mirror lines on templates.

To cut a perfect miter on a strip no wider than 3", turn the Perfect Piecer so that the 90 degree angle is facing straight up and the miter line is horizontal. Line the miter line up with the bottom edge of the border strip. Move the Perfect Piecer to the spot where the miter is to be cut and draw along the right hand edge of the Piecer. Cut the miter.

To cut miters on border strips wider than 3", a larger right triangle would work better.

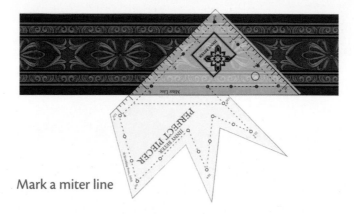

Mark a miter line

To use the Perfect Piecer as a right triangle for marking mirror lines on triangle templates, use the 90 degree angle. Place the bottom of the Perfect Piecer along the bottom of the template and move the Piecer to the left until the 45 degree angle touches the tip of the triangle. Then draw the miter line down the middle of the template.

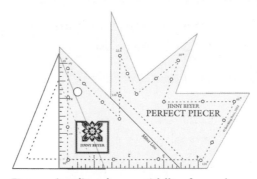

Draw miter line down middle of template

Sewing the Blocks

When assembling blocks, keep in mind these basic rules:

- Combine smaller pieces to make larger units
- Join larger units into rows or sections
- Join sections to complete blocks

If you follow these rules, you will be able to build most blocks using only straight seams.

Each pattern has illustrations showing how to assemble the blocks. For most blocks, the pieces can be sewn together with all straight lines. A few of the blocks have set-in seams. These are not hard to do. For these seams, stitching must start and stop at the place where the seam allowances come together. This will result in a Y seam that will allow the set in piece. The templates, where a Y seam is involved are marked with small dots. These are the start and stopping spots.

Two of the blocks have some curved seams. When sewing curves, I like to have the concave (inward curve) piece on the top. To avoid puckers, sew an exact quarter inch seam (see Jinny Beyer Perfect Piecer on page 12).

Assembling the Blocks

Once all the blocks have been sewn, assemble them in the modules that were discussed on page 1. Use the quilt illustration on page iv for placement of the blocks. Each module has two small, two medium, and one large sized block.

1. Make three rectangular templates for the sashing in the following sizes:

    Sashing Template A: $1\frac{5}{8}$" x 6 $\frac{7}{8}$" for the sashing between the small blocks
    Sashing Template B: $1\frac{5}{8}$" x $10\frac{5}{8}$" for the sashing between the medium-sized blocks
    Sashing Template C: $1\frac{5}{8}$" x $14\frac{3}{8}$" for the sashing between the large blocks and the small ones.

2. Find the middle of the templates and mark mirror lines.

3. From the reserved $1\frac{5}{8}$" x $10\frac{1}{2}$ yard pieces of narrow border stripe, cut the following pieces, beginning with the longest and cutting the shortest last:

    Cut one $1\frac{5}{8}$" x $51\frac{3}{8}$" piece with a mirror image motif from the border centered in the middle of the strip.
    Cut six $1\frac{5}{8}$" by $21\frac{7}{8}$" strips, again centering a design in the middle of the strips.
    Cut four identical pieces each from sashing templates A, B and C. Use the mirror lines on the templates to center the same design from the border in the middle of the templates.

4. Lay out the blocks according the modules shown on page 1. Begin by sewing sashing strip A between two of the smallest blocks in the first module. Sew a sashing strip C to the long side of these blocks and then sew a large block to sashing strip C.

5. Sew two of the medium sized blocks together with sashing strip B in between them. Sew a $21\frac{7}{8}$" sashing strip to these blocks and then join this to the rest of the module. Make all four modules.

6. Join Module 1 and 2 with a $21\frac{7}{8}$" strip of sashing between them. Do the same for Modules 3 and 4. Join the two sets of modules together with the 51 $\frac{3}{8}$" strip of sashing between.

ADDING THE BORDERS

Golden Album Quilt is rectangular. You may, however, choose to select just one of the blocks in this book and repeat that for a quilt. The quilt may end up being square or rectangular. Therefore, instructions are given here for adding borders to a square or a rectangular quilt.

I like to measure and sew the third border separately after the first two borders are complete. The reason for adding the border print pieces separately is to assure that the miters will come out exactly the same at the edges.

FRAMING SQUARE QUILTS WITH BORDER PRINT FABRIC

If the quilt is square it is quite easy to cut the strips and have perfectly mitered corners.

1. Smooth the quilt out on a carpet, then place a strip of the border print across the *middle* of the quilt, centering the mirror-imaged motif from the border-print strip at the exact center of the piece. Centering this mirror-imaged motif in the middle of the quilt, assures that the design on the border print where it comes to either edge of the quilt will be the same.

Step 1

2. Use a right-angle 45-degree triangle to mark the miter along one of the edges. Position the triangle so that one of the short sides of the right angle runs along the bottom edge of the border print. Then carefully move the triangle until the angled portion touches the place where the top edge of the border print meets the edge of the quilt. Mark, then cut the miter. Since you have cut the miter right at the edge of the quilt, the seam allowance will already be included.

Step 2

3. Without disturbing the entire strip of border, carefully pick up the mitered edge and fold it over to the other end of the border strip at the opposite side of the quilt. Position it at the point where the miter will be, making sure that the design on the fabric matches. (If you correctly centered the motif in the middle of the quilt in step 1, the designs should match perfectly at the edges.) Cut the second miter.

Step 3

4. Using this first mitered piece as a "pattern," place it on additional strips of border print fabric, matching the design exactly. Cut three more identical pieces, making sure that the design on the border print is exactly the same on all four pieces.

Step 4

Complete

Repeat this process for any additional borders that are to be added to the quilt. Note that the measurements for your fabric strips reserved for borders have allowed for extra length. This is to accommodate any variation in size of the overall quilt as well as to make it possible to manipulate the fabric in order for a mirror-imaged motif to be centered in the middle of the quilt.

Framing Rectangular Quilts with Border Print Fabric

Not all quilts are as easy to border as those that are square. Yet it is still a relatively simple process to assure that the miters will match perfectly on quilts that are longer than they are wide. There is just one extra step involved. First, you will need to measure and cut the two shorter sides exactly as described above. The other two sides are cut differently. Each side is, in fact, made up of two mirror-imaged pieces, each one with a mitered edge. The miters are cut to match the miters of the first two previously cut sides, then the two "mirrored pieces" meet at the middle of the quilt to form their own mirror-imaged motifs.

There are three borders on *Golden Album Quilt*. The first is the narrow border stripe from the border print. The second border is a coordinating fabric and the third is the wide stripe from the border print. I prefer adding each border individually. Some people prefer sewing the three strips together and treating them as one. If you do this you have to make sure that a mirror imaged motif from both Border 1 and 3 are in the same places at the middle of the strips.

Follow these steps for adding the borders to *Golden Album Quilt*.

1. Working with the two reserved 1 ½ yard narrow strips of border print (Border 1), measure and cut the miters for the two short sides of the quilt. Follow steps 1-4 above.

2. There will be two pieces for each of the long sides of the quilt. Place the mitered edge of one of the pieces cut for the short sides of the quilt onto one of the reserved 1 yard pieces of narrow border print. Making sure the design motifs match perfectly, cut the miter edge to match. Place the newly cut strip along the length of the quilt (through the middle, not at the edge). The mitered edge is positioned at the edge of the quilt as shown here. Bring the strip to the exact center of the quilt, mark this center on the mitered strip and then cut ¼" beyond the center. This will allow for seam allowance when two mirror-imaged strips are sewn together.

Step 2

3. Using this cut strip as a guide, lay it on another of the 1 yard strips and, carefully matching the design, cut one more piece identical to it. Next cut two strips that are the exact mirror images of the first piece. The easiest way to get the mirror-imaged pieces is to place one of the already cut strips upside down on one of the 1 yard strips. Match the designs exactly and cut to match.

4. Sew pairs of mirror-image strips together to make two long border strips. The mirror-image motif at the center of each will disguise the seam.

Step 4

5. Sew these Border 1 strips to the quilt, following the directions below, then repeat the process for Borders 2 and 3. Note that Border 2 does not require center seams because it is not a border print fabric. See the note on grain on page 4.

Seam here

Seam here

Step 5

SEWING BORDERS ONTO THE QUILT

Due to possible stretching at the seams and also bias-stretch, the edges of a quilt top are often longer than the measurements through the middle of the quilt. Since borders are correctly cut to middle-of-quilt measurements, you may end up with border strips that are slightly shorter than the quilt edge. This means that when you sew the borders on, the quilt edges will have to be eased back to their proper size. Follow these steps.

1. Since the angle of the mitered border strip is not the same as the right angle of the corner of the quilt, it is best to mark with a dot where the seam allowances will cross. Using the 90 degree angle on the Jinny Beyer Perfect Piecer, mark the corner of the quilt. Use the 135 degree angle to mark the angle of the border print.

2. Working with the border print strip on top, begin by pinning the mid-point of one of the border pieces to the middle of one of the edges of the quilt.

3. Matching the dots on the quilt and the border strip, pin the corners next. Whether you are sewing by hand or by machine, the stitching will stop at these dots.

4. Now, by folding, find the mid-point of the quilt and the border strip between each of the two halves and pin those together. Continue finding the mid-points between pins and continue pinning. Ease in any fullness.

5. With the border print on top, carefully sew the seam just next to the line on the border print, easing in any extra fullness, starting and ending at the dots. Sew each of the border strips in this manner.

6. If the border has mitered edges, pin the miters carefully together, making sure not to stretch the bias edges. If the strips are border prints, make sure the design on the miters exactly matches and pin securely. Because of the length of bias miters, the pieces can become slightly distorted and stretched. I take one additional step that will remedy any distortion that may have occurred.

Once the miters are sewn, lay the corner, right side up, on the ironing board so that there is at least 12" of border print on the ironing board on either side of the mitered corner. Reach underneath and gently push the seam allowances to one side or the other. Then use the iron to make a more accurate miter seam line to sew on. Softly run the iron over the seam, pushing in the direction *away from* the seam allowance. If there is any extra fullness in the miter, the iron will press it in place and make the corner perfectly square. Stitch the portion of the miter along the crease left by the iron.

Prepare for Quilting

After the quilt top is assembled, clip any dangling threads and then press the quilt top carefully. I never press seams open. Iron the seams of the sashing strips *away from* the sashing. This will make it easier to quilt some type of design in the sashing strips. Press seams of all the borders in one direction.

Layer the backing, batting and quilt top and baste all three layers together. Typically, working from the center, I first baste diagonally from corner to corner.

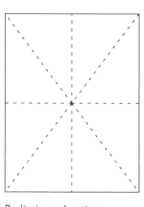

Preliminary basting

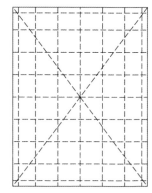

Basting grid

Then I baste both vertically and horizontally through the center of the quilt, and finally I create a grid with no more than an 8" square unbasted.

Quilting

I am a traditionalist when it comes to the quilting design and prefer to quilt a little over ¼" from the seam (just beyond the seam allowance) around each of the shapes in the patchwork block. The exception is the pieces that have been cut from the border print. Then I like to enhance the design on the fabric by quilting around a motif in the fabric.

For the sashing and borders I follow lines on the border print. Border 2 could be quilted with a decorative motif, straight lines or whatever you choose.

Binding the Quilt

There are various methods of finishing off the edges once the quilting is complete. The most popular method (and the one I prefer) is a cut binding that is added around the quilt to finish off the raw edges. Binding can be cut from straight pieces of fabric or it can be cut on the bias. I prefer binding cut on the bias for two reasons. First, I think it gives a smoother finish to the edges of the quilt and, second, I believe bias is more durable over time. The edges of the quilt are going to get the most wear. Straight grain binding is folded along one continuous thread, creating a weakness that can cause it to wear and fray much more quickly. With bias binding, if a thread gets frayed, it will only go at a diagonal a short distance. To make the binding even more durable, I usually cut it twice as wide as the finished width, plus seam allowance, then I double it over.

CUTTING THE BINDING

For this double-fold bias binding, you will need to cut strips of fabric four times the desired finished width of the binding, plus the seam allowance. Most quilters cut their binding somewhere between 2" and 2 ½" wide. Here is the method I use.

1. Begin with at least ½ to 1 yard of fabric. Remove the selvage from both sides, fold the fabric in half on the diagonal, and press.

2. Cut along the fold, but leave the two pieces aligned. Using a see-through ruler and a piece of tailor's chalk, mark cutting lines, the desired width, along the diagonal on the top piece of fabric. Cut through both layers.

3. With right sides facing, use a ¼" seam allowance to sew the binding strips together at their ends. Since the strips have been cut all the way to the edge of the fabric, their ends should be at the correct angle.

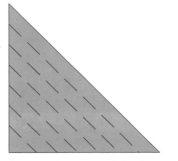

Step 2: Cut through both layers

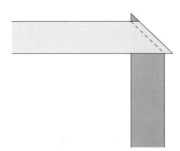

Step: 3 Ends will be at correct angle for easy sewing

ATTACHING THE BINDING

The conventional way of adding binding is to sew it to the front of the quilt and then bring it to the back and stitch it down in an invisible hem stitch. When a border print stripe is used as the final border around the outside of the quilt, I do the opposite. In order for the seam to look even, it is important to sew the binding directly to a line along the border print. Therefore I pin the binding to the back of the quilt, sew the binding first to the back and then bring it to the front. I use a small blind stitch and sew it alongside the edge of a line on the border print.

1. For double-fold binding, fold the long binding strip in half lengthwise, wrong sides together, and gently press, making sure that the bias edges do not stretch.

2. Beginning along one side of the quilt, align the raw edges of the binding along the edge of the wrong side of the quilt. Pin the binding to the quilt, leaving an approximate 5" "tail." Pin small sections at a time.

3. Working with the front side of the quilt facing you, but with the binding pinned to the back, sew ¼" from the edge, stitching just outside a line on the border print design, if there is one.

4. As you approach a corner, stop stitching ¼" from the edge and take a back stitch. Fold the binding strip up at a 45-degree angle. Fold the strip back down so there is a crease at the upper edge. Insert the needle through the base of the fold and continue sewing down the next side. (Note that the drawings are for hand-sewing the binding. If you are working by machine, the quilt must be removed from the machine in order to fold the binding up then down before you continue stitching.)

5. When you are approximately 8" from the original starting point, take the piece you are currently sewing and bring it over to meet the 5" tail. Cut off the excess binding, allowing enough length to connect the two ends and have a 5" overlap (it is better to cut it too long than too short). Cut the binding to match the angle of the original tail. Fold under ¼" of the cut-off end and press. Slip the raw edges of the 5" tail inside the folded edges. Blind stitch the ends together.

6. Carefully pin and sew this last bit of binding down.

7. Bring the binding over to the front of the quilt and blind stitch the folded edge in place along the line of the border print, covering the first set of stitches with the folded edge. At the corners fold in the adjacent sides to form a miter. Take several stitches in the miter on both sides of the quilt.

Step 4: Fold up at 45° angle

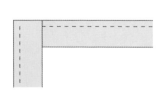

Step 5: Fold strip back down

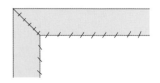

Step 7: At corner fold adjacent sides to form miter

1. Windmill

Only three pattern pieces are needed for this block. Be sure to cut the border print pieces (A) so that a mirror image motif is centered in the middle of the triangle (use *mirror line* on template as a guide). Also, be sure that a line from the border print falls just within the seam line so that it will show in the completed block.

Ladies Art Company, 1897

Block Assembly

UNIT 1: Sew two Template A triangles together, one cut from Fabric 1 and the other cut from Fabric 6. Make four.

UNIT 2: Sew two Template B triangles cut from Fabric 12 to a Template C square cut from Fabric 6. Make four.

UNIT 3: Sew a Unit 1 piece to a Unit 2 piece. Make four.

UNIT 4: Sew two Unit 3 pieces together, orienting the units as shown. Make two.

FINISHED BLOCK: Sew two Unit 4 pieces together, orienting the units as shown.

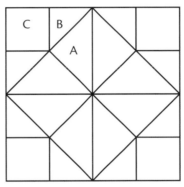

Template guide
(see page 61)

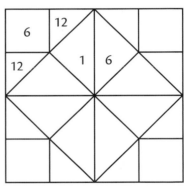

Fabric guide
(see chart on page 3)

Unit 1: Make four

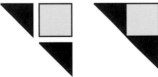

Unit 2: Make four

Unit 3: Make four

Unit 4: Make two

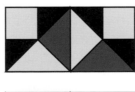

Complete block

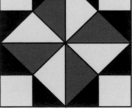

2. Mosaic No. 2

(6⅜" Block)

Ladies Art Company, 1897

Only three pattern pieces are needed for *Mosaic No. 2*. Be sure to cut the border print pieces (C) so that a mirror image motif is centered in the middle of the piece (use *mirror line* on template as a guide). Also, be sure that a line from the border print falls just within the seam line so that it will show in the completed block.

Block Assembly

UNIT 1: Sew two Template A triangles together, one cut from Fabric 8 and the other cut from Fabric 10. Make four.

UNIT 2: Sew two Unit 1 squares together, orienting them as shown. Make two.

UNIT 3: Sew two Unit 2 pieces together to form a square. Make one.

UNIT 4: Sew a Template A triangle cut from Fabric 11 to a border print piece cut from Template C. Make four.

UNIT 5: Sew four Template B triangles cut from Fabric 10 to Unit 3. Make one.

FINISHED BLOCK: Sew the four Unit 4 pieces to Unit 5 to complete the block.

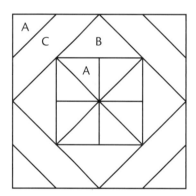

Template guide
(see page 62)

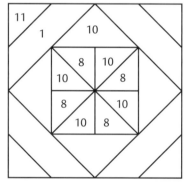

Fabric guide
(see chart on page 3)

Unit 1: Make four

Unit 2: Make two

Unit 3: Make one

Unit 4: Make four

Unit 5: Make one

Complete block

3. Double Wrench

Only two pattern pieces are needed for this block. Be sure to cut the border print pieces (A and B) so that a mirror image motif is centered in the middle of the piece (use *mirror line* on template as a guide). Also, be sure that a line from the border print falls just within the seam line so that it will show in the completed block.

Ladies Art Company, 1897

Block Assembly

UNIT 1: Sew two Template A squares together, one cut from Fabric 1 and the other cut from Fabric 3, orienting the pieces as shown. Make four.

UNIT 2: Sew two Unit 1 pieces to a square cut from Fabric 3, orienting them as in the diagram. Make one.

UNIT 3: Sew two B triangles together, one cut from Fabric 1 and the other cut from Fabric 3. Make four.

UNIT 4: Sew two Unit 3 pieces to either side of a Unit 1 piece. Orient the pieces as shown. Make two.

FINISHED BLOCK: Sew two Unit 4 pieces to the Unit 2 piece, as shown.

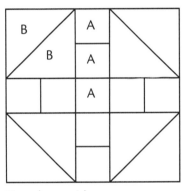

Template guide
(see page 63)

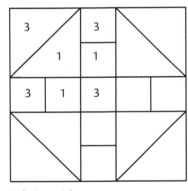

Fabric guide
(see chart on page 3)

Unit 1: Make four

Unit 2: Make one

Unit 3: Make four

Unit 4: Make two

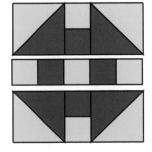 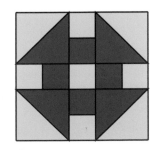

Complete block

4. Sawtooth Patchwork

(6⅜" Block)

Ladies Art Company, 1897

Three pattern pieces are needed for *Sawtooth Patchwork.* Be sure to cut the border print pieces (C) so that a mirror image motif is centered in the middle of the triangle (use *mirror line* on template as a guide). Also, be sure that a line from the border print falls just within the seam line along the long side of the triangle so that it will show in the completed block.

Block Assembly

UNIT 1: Sew two Template C triangles together, one cut from Fabric 1 and the other cut from Fabric 6. Make four.

UNIT 2: Sew four Template B triangles cut from Fabric 6 to a square cut from Fabric 10. Make five.

UNIT 3: Sew three Unit 2 squares together. Make one.

UNIT 4: Sew a Unit 1 piece to either side of a Unit 2 square. Orient the pieces as shown. Make two.

FINISHED BLOCK: Sew two Unit 4 pieces to the Unit 3 piece to complete the block.

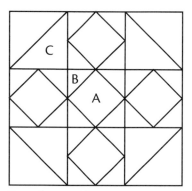

Template guide
(see page 64)

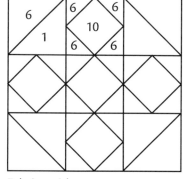

Fabric guide
(see chart on page 3)

Unit 1: Make four

Unit 2: Make five

Unit 3: Make one

Unit 4: Make two

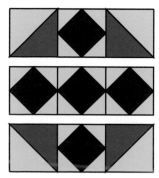

Complete block

5. Card Trick

Three pattern pieces are needed for *Card Trick*. Be sure to cut the border print pieces (B and C) so that a mirror image motif is centered in the middle of the triangle (use *mirror line* on template as a guide). Also, be sure that a line from the border print falls just within the seam line so that it will show in the completed block.

Block Assembly

UNIT 1: Sew two Template B triangles together, one cut from Fabric 1 and the other cut from Fabric 11. Make four.

UNIT 2: Sew two Template C triangles together, one cut from Fabric 1, and one cut from Fabric 11. Make four.

UNIT 3: Sew a Unit 2 piece to a B triangle cut from Fabric 1. Make four.

UNIT 4: Sew two Unit 3 pieces to either side of a square cut from Fabric 12. Orient the pieces as shown. Make one.

UNIT 5: Sew a Unit 1 piece to ether side of a Unit 3 piece, orienting the pieces as shown. Make two.

FINISHED BLOCK: Sew two Unit 5 pieces to the Unit 4 piece to complete the block.

Beth Gutcheon, *The Perfect Patchwork Primer,* 1973

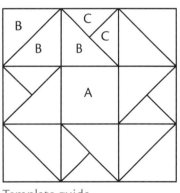

Template guide
(see page 65)

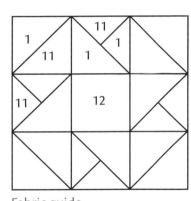

Fabric guide
(see chart on page 3)

Unit 1: Make four

Unit 2: Make four

Unit 3: Make four

Unit 4: Make one

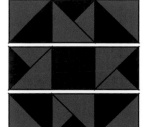 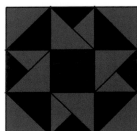

Complete block

Unit 5: Make two

6. Basket Quilt

(6⅜" Block)

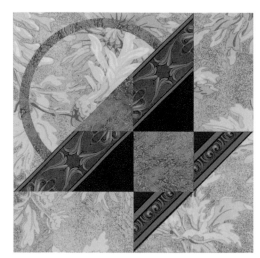

Ladies Art Company, 1897

Six different pattern pieces are required for *Basket Quilt.* It is a block that is sewn with both appliqué and piecing techniques. The handle of the basket is appliquéd onto the large Template D triangle. Cut the border print pieces (B and C) so that a mirror image motif is centered in the middle of the pieces (use *mirror line* on templates as a guide). Also be sure that a line from the border print falls just within the seam line so that it will show in the completed block.

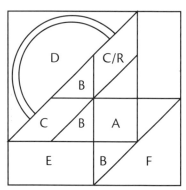

Template guide
(see page 66)

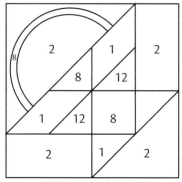

Fabric guide
(see chart on page 3)

Block Assembly

UNIT 1: Turn under ⅛" on either side of the bias piece cut for the handle. Then, using the curved lines on Template D as a guide, appliqué the handle to the triangle. Make one.

UNIT 2: Sew a Template C piece to a Template B triangle cut from Fabric 12. Make one and one reversed.

UNIT 3: Sew a Unit 2 piece to a Template E rectangle. Make one and one reversed.

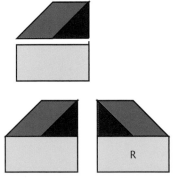

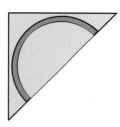

Unit 1: Make one

Unit 2: Make one and one R

Unit 3: Make one and one R

UNIT 4: Sew two Template B triangles cut from Fabric 1 to the Template A square. Make one.

UNIT 5: Sew the Template F triangle to Unit 4. Make one.

UNIT 6: Sew a Template B triangle cut from Fabric 8 to reversed Unit 3. Make one.

UNIT 7: Sew Unit 3 (not reversed) to Unit 5. Make one.

UNIT 8: Sew Unit 6 to Unit 7. Make one.

FINISHED BLOCK: Sew Unit 1 to Unit 8 to complete the block.

Unit 4: Make one

Unit 5: Make one

Unit 6: Make one

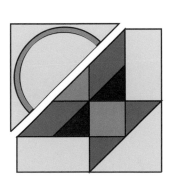

Unit 7: Make one

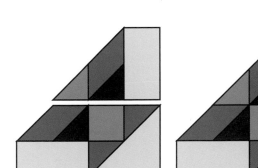

Unit 8: Make one

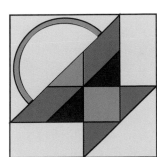

Complete block

Johnnie Around the Corner

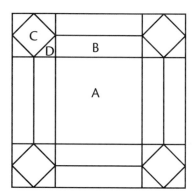

Ladies Art Company, 1973

Four pattern pieces are needed for *Johnnie Around the Corner*. Cut four identical border print pieces (B) so that a mirror image motif is centered in the middle of the rectangle (use *mirror line* on template as a guide). Also, be sure that a line from the border print falls just within the seam line so that it will show in the completed block.

Block Assembly

UNIT 1: Sew four Template D triangles around square C. Make four.

UNIT 2: Sew two Template B rectangles together, one cut from Fabric 1 and one cut from Fabric 2. Make four.

UNIT 3: Sew two Unit 2 pieces to opposite sides of large square A. Make one.

UNIT 4: Sew two Unit 1 pieces to either side of a Unit 2 piece, orienting them as shown. Make two.

FINISHED BLOCK: Sew the two Unit 4 pieces to the Unit 3 piece to complete the block.

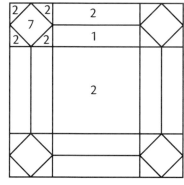

Template guide
(see page 67)

Fabric guide
(see chart on page 3)

Unit 1: Make four

Unit 2: Make four

Unit 3: Make one

Unit 4: Make two

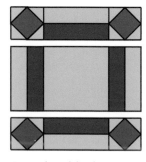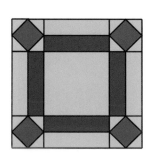

Complete block

8. The House That Jack Built

Four pattern pieces are needed for *The House That Jack Built*. Cut eight identical border print pieces (B) so that a mirror image motif is centered in the middle of the rectangle (use *mirror line* on template as a guide). Also, be sure that a line from the border print falls just within the seam line so that it will show in the completed block.

Ladies Art Company, 1897

Block Assembly

UNIT 1: Sew three Template B rectangles together, two cut from Fabric 1 and one cut from Fabric 4. Make four.

UNIT 2: Sew a D triangle along the long side of one of the Fabric 1 pieces in Unit 1. Make four.

UNIT 3: Sew two Unit 2 pieces to opposite sides of large square A. Make one.

UNIT 4: Sew a D triangle to either side of a Unit 2 piece, orienting them as shown. Make two.

FINISHED BLOCK: Sew two Unit 4 pieces to the Unit 3 piece to complete the block.

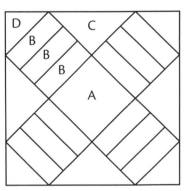

Template guide
(see page 68)

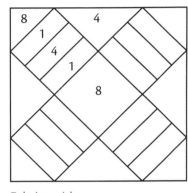

Fabric guide
(see chart on page 3)

Unit 1: Make four

Unit 2: Make four   Unit 3: Make one

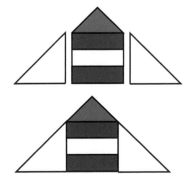

Unit 4: Make two

Complete block

9. Lost Ship Pattern

(6⅜" Block)

Ladies Art Company, 1897

Only two pattern pieces are needed for *Lost Ship Pattern*. Cut the border print triangles (A) so that a mirror image motif is centered in the middle of the template (use *mirror line* on template as a guide). Also be sure that a line from the border print falls just within the seam line so that it will show in the completed block.

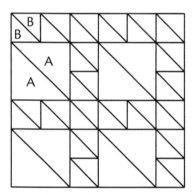

Template guide
(see page 69)

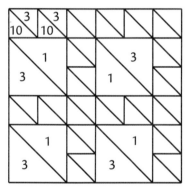

Fabric guide
(see chart on page 3)

Block Assembly

UNIT 1: Sew two Template B triangles together, one cut from Fabric 3 and one cut from Fabric 10. Make 20.

UNIT 2: Sew two Template A triangles together, one cut from Fabric 1 and one cut from Fabric 3. Make four.

UNIT 3: Sew two Unit 1 pieces together. Make four.

UNIT 4: Sew a Unit 3 piece to a Unit 2 piece as shown. Make three.

Unit 1: Make 20

Unit 2: Make four

Unit 3: Make four

Unit 4: Make three

UNIT 5: Sew a Unit 3 to a Unit 2, as shown. Make one.

UNIT 6: Sew two Unit 4 pieces together. Make one.

UNIT 7: Sew a Unit 4 piece to the Unit 5 piece. Make one

UNIT 8: Sew six Unit 1 pieces together. Make two.

UNIT 9: Sew the Unit 6 piece to one of the Unit 8 pieces. Make one.

UNIT 10: Sew the Unit 7 piece to one of the Unit 8 pieces. Make one.

FINISHED BLOCK: Sew Unit 9 and Unit 10 together as shown.

Unit 5: Make one

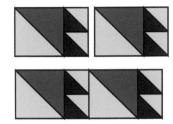

Unit 6: Make one

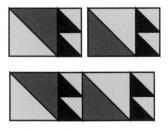

Unit 7: Make one

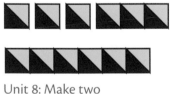

Unit 8: Make two

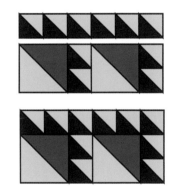

Unit 9: Make one

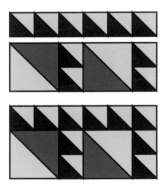

Unit 10: Make one

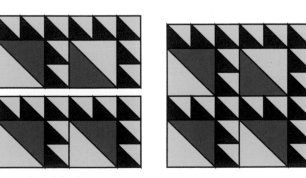

Complete block

10. Lily Quilt Pattern

(10⅛" Block)

Ladies Art Company, 1897

Seven pattern pieces are needed for *Lily Quilt Pattern*. Be sure to cut the border print pieces (A, B, and C) so that a mirror image motif is centered in the middle of the piece (use *mirror line* on template as a guide). Also, be sure that a line from the border print falls just within the seam line so that it will show in the completed block.

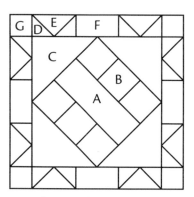

Template guide
(see page 70)

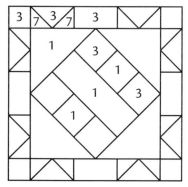

Fabric guide
(see chart on page 3)

Block Assembly

UNIT 1: Sew three Template B squares together, one cut from Fabric 1 and two cut from Fabric 3. Make two.

UNIT 2: Sew a Unit 1 strip to either side of the Template A rectangle. Make one.

UNIT 3: Sew four Template C triangles to Unit 2, as shown. Make one.

Unit 1: Make two

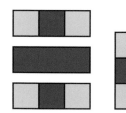

Unit 2: Make one

Unit 3: Make one, orienting as shown.

UNIT 4: Sew the long side of two Template D triangles to the short sides of a Template E triangle. Make eight.

UNIT 5: Sew a Unit 4 piece to either side of a Template F rectangle. Make four.

UNIT 6: Sew a Template G square to either side of a Unit 5 piece. Make two.

UNIT 7: Sew the two Unit 5 pieces to opposite sides of the Unit 3 piece, orienting as shown. Make one.

FINISHED BLOCK: Sew two Unit 6 pieces to opposite sides of Unit 7 to complete the block.

Unit 4: Make eight

Unit 5: Make four

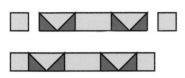

Unit 6: Make two

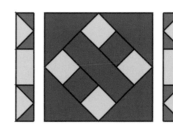 

Unit 7: Make one

Complete block

11. Burnham Square

(10⅛" Block)

Ladies Art Company, 1897

Six pattern pieces are needed for *Burnham Square*. Cut identical border print pieces (E) and center a mirror image motif in the middle of the rectangle (use *mirror line* on template as a guide). Also, be sure that a line from the border print falls just within the seam line so that it will show in the completed block.

Template guide
(see page 71)

Fabric guide
(see chart on page 3)

Block Assembly

UNIT 1: Sew two Template F triangles together, one cut from Fabric 3 and one cut from Fabric 10. Make four.

UNIT 2: Sew three Template E rectangles together, two cut from Fabric 1 and one cut from Fabric 8. Make four.

UNIT 3: Sew a Unit 1 square to either side of a Unit 2 piece. Make two.

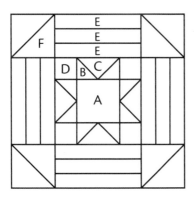

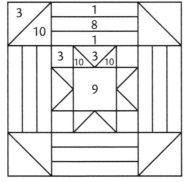

Unit 1: Make four

Unit 2: Make four

Unit 3: Make two

UNIT 4: Sew a Template B triangle to either side of a Template C triangle. Make four.

UNIT 5: Sew a Template D square to either side of a Unit four piece. Make two.

UNIT 6: Sew a Unit 4 piece to either side of the center square A. Make one.

UNIT 7: Sew a Unit 5 piece to either side the Unit 6 piece. Make one.

UNIT 8: Sew two Unit 2 pieces to opposite sides of Unit 7. Make one.

FINISHED BLOCK. Sew two Unit 3 pieces to Unit 8 to complete the block.

Unit 4: Make four

Unit 5: Make two

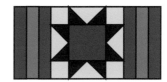

Unit 6: Make one

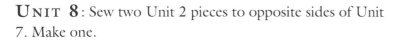
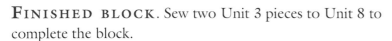

Unit 7: Make one

Unit 8: Make two

Complete block

12. The Prosperity Block

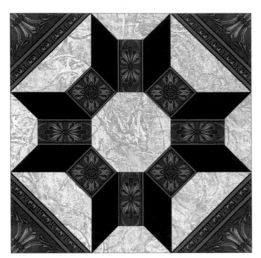

Quilt Booklet No. 1, 1922

Seven pattern pieces are needed for *The Prosperity Block*. From border print fabric, cut 16 identical Template B triangles, four identical Template C rectangles, and four identical Template F triangles. On all of these Fabric 1 pieces, cut so that a mirror image motif is centered in the middle of the piece (use *mirror line* on templates as a guide). Also, be sure that a line from the border print falls just within the seam line so that it will show in the completed block. Use the Jinny Beyer Perfect Piecer, as described on page 13, to mark the stopping points and pivot places for the points and the set-in seams.

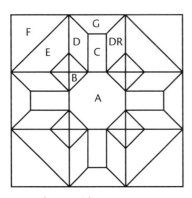

Template guide
(see page 72)

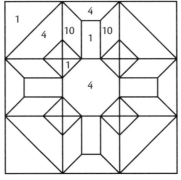

Fabric guide
(see chart on page 3)

Block Assembly

UNIT 1: Sew a Template F triangle and a Template B triangle to piece E. Make four.

UNIT 2: Sew a Template B triangle to a Template D piece. Sew another Template B triangle to a reversed Template D piece. Make four each.

UNIT 3: Sew a Unit 2 and a Unit 2 reversed to the long sides of a Template C piece. At the top, stitch only to the seam allowances (dot) to allow for a Y seam for setting in the next piece (see page 15). Make four.

Unit 1: Make four

Unit 2: Make four each

Unit 3: Make four

UNIT 4: Set in a Template G piece to Unit 3, pivoting at the Y seams. Make four.

UNIT 5: Sew four Template B triangles to the center octagon A. Make one.

UNIT 6: Sew two Unit 4 pieces to opposite sides of Unit 5. Make one.

UNIT 7: Sew two Unit 1 pieces to opposite sides of Unit 4. Make two.

FINISHED BLOCK: Sew two Unit 7 pieces to Unit 6 to complete the block.

Unit 4: Make four

Unit 5: Make one

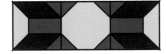

Unit 6: Make one

Unit 7: Make two

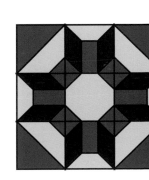

Complete block

13. Cross and Crown

The Country Gentleman, July 1930

Seven pattern pieces are needed for *Cross and Crown*. Cut the Template C triangles so that a mirror image motif is centered in the middle of the piece (use *mirror line* on templates as a guide). Also, be sure that a line from the border print falls just within the seam line so that it will show in the completed block.

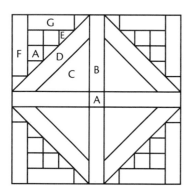

Template guide
(see page 73)

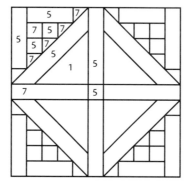

Fabric guide
(see chart on page 3)

Block Assembly

UNIT 1: Sew three Template A squares and three Template E triangles together in rows as shown. Make four.

UNIT 2: Sew a Template E triangle to a Template F rectangle. Make two and two reversed.

UNIT 3: Sew a Template E triangle to a Template G rectangle. Make two and two reversed.

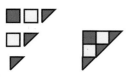

Unit 1: Make four

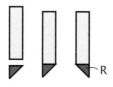

Unit 2: Make two
and two reveresed

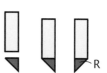

Unit 3: Make two
and two reversed

UNIT 4: Sew Unit 3 to Unit 1. Make two and two reversed.

UNIT 5: Sew Unit 2 to Unit 4. Make two and two reversed.

UNIT 6: Sew Unit 5 and a Template C triangle to a Template D piece. Make two and two reversed.

UNIT 7: Sew two Template B rectangles to opposite sides of a Template A square. Make one.

UNIT 8: Sew Unit 6 and Unit 6 reversed to opposite sides of a Template B rectangle. Make two.

FINISHED BLOCK: Sew two Unit 8 pieces to Unit 7 to complete the block.

Unit 4: Make two and two reversed

Unit 5: Make two and two reversed

Unit 6: Make two and two reversed

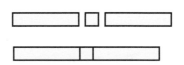

Unit 7: Make one

Unit 8: Make two

Complete block

14. Imperial T

(10⅛" Block)

Ladies Art Company, 1897

Seven pattern pieces are needed for *Imperial T*. Cut the Template B and F triangles so that a mirror image motif is centered in the middle of the piece (use *mirror line* on templates as a guide). The Template D triangles are *not* centered over a mirror image; they must match at the miter with the design on the Template F pieces. On all pieces cut from border print Fabric 1, be sure that a line from the border print falls just within the seam line so that it will show in the completed block.

Template guide
(see page 74)

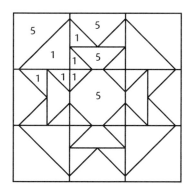

Fabric guide
(see chart on page 3)

Block Assembly

UNIT 1: Sew a Template G piece and a Template F triangle together. Make four.

UNIT 2: Sew two Template D triangles to a Template E piece. Make four.

UNIT 3: Sew two Template B triangles to a Template C piece. Make four.

Unit 1: Make four

Unit 2: Make four

Unit 3: Make four

UNIT 4: Sew Unit 2 to Unit 3. Make four.

UNIT 5: Sew two Unit 1 pieces to opposite sides of Unit 4, orienting them as shown. Make two.

UNIT 6: Sew four Template B triangles to the Template A piece. Make one.

UNIT 7: Sew two Unit 4 pieces to opposite sides of Unit 6, orienting the pieces as shown. Make one.

FINISHED BLOCK: Sew two Unit 5 pieces to Unit 7 to complete the block.

Unit 4: Make four

Unit 5: Make two

Unit 6: Make one

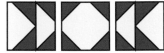

Unit 7: Make one

Complete block

15. The Royal

(10⅛" Block)

Ladies Art Company, 1897

Six pattern pieces are needed for *The Royal*. Cut the Template C pieces so that a mirror image motif is centered in the middle of the piece (use *mirror line* on templates as a guide). On all Template C pieces cut from border print Fabric 1, be sure that a line from the border print falls just within the seam line so that it will show in the completed block.

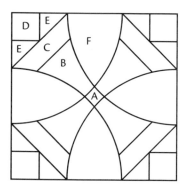

Template guide
(see page 75)

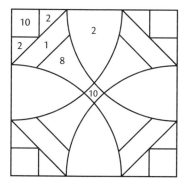

Fabric guide
(see chart on page 3)

Block Assembly

UNIT 1: Sew two Template E triangles to a Template D square. Make four.

UNIT 2: Sew a Template B piece and a Template C piece together. Make four.

UNIT 3: Sew Unit 1 to Unit 2. Make four.

Unit 1: Make four

Unit 2: Make four

Unit 3: Make four

UNIT 4: Sew two Unit 3 sections to opposite sides of the Template A piece. Make one.

UNIT 5: Sew two Template F pieces to Unit 3 as shown. Make two.

FINISHED BLOCK: Sew two Unit 5 pieces to Unit 4 to complete the block.

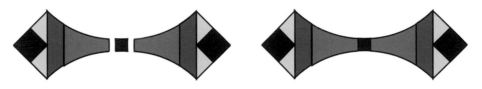

Unit 4: Make one

Unit 5: Make two

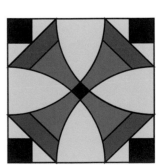

Complete block

16. Arrant Red Birds

(10⅛" Block)

Nancy Cabot, *Chicago Tribune,* Jan 2, 1936

Five pattern pieces are needed for *Arrant Red Birds.* Mark the templates for triangles B and D carefully. They are similar, but are not the same size. Carefully cut the Template C and E pieces from border print Fabric 1 so that a mirror image motif is centered in the middle of the piece (use *mirror line* on templates as a guide). On all pieces cut from border print Fabric 1, be sure that a line from the border print falls just within the seam line so that it will show in the completed block. Use the Jinny Beyer Perfect Piecer as described on page 13 to mark the stopping points and pivot places for the points and set-in seams.

Template guide
(see page 76)

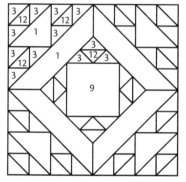

Fabric guide
(see chart on page 3)

Block Assembly

UNIT 1: Sew two Template B triangles together, one cut from Fabric 12 and one cut from Fabric 3. Make four.

UNIT 2: Sew two Template B triangles cut from Fabric 3 to Unit 1. Make four.

UNIT 3: Sew four Unit 2 triangles to the center square A. Make one.

Unit 1: Make four

Unit 2: Make four

Unit 3: Make one

Unit 4: Sew two Template D triangles together, one cut from Fabric 12 and one cut from Fabric 3. Make twelve.

Unit 5: Sew two Template D triangles cut from Fabric 3 to Unit 4. Make twelve.

Unit 6: Sew a Template E triangle to Unit 5. Make four.

Unit 7: Sew two Unit 5 pieces to Unit 6. Make four.

Unit 8: Sew four Template C pieces to Unit 3. Make one.

Finished block: Sew four Unit 7 pieces to Unit 8 to complete the block.

Unit 4: Make twelve

Unit 5: Make twelve

Unit 6: Make four

 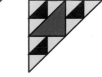

Unit 7: Make four

Unit 8: Make one

Complete block

17. New Millenium

(13⅞" Block)

Jinny Beyer, Hilton Head Seminar design, 1999

Five pattern pieces (two of them reversed) are needed for *New Millennium*. Because of the way the Template C pieces are cut from the border print fabric, it appears that there are more fabrics than one in that piece. Cut these pieces so that a mirror image motif is centered in the middle of the template (use *mirror line* as a guide). Use the Jinny Beyer Perfect Piecer, as described on page 13, to mark the stopping points and pivot places for the points and the set-in seams. Note that Template D looks symmetrical, but it is not. That is why reversed pieces are required.

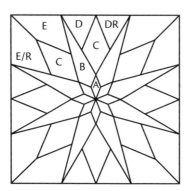

Template guide
(see page 77)

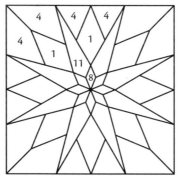

Fabric guide
(see chart on page 3)

Block Assembly

UNIT 1: Sew three Template A diamonds together, then add a fourth diamond. Make two.

UNIT 2: Sew the two Unit 1 pieces together. Make one.

UNIT 3: Sew four Template B points into Unit 2. Make one.

Unit 1: Make two

Unit 2: Make one

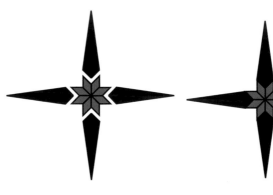

Unit 3: Make one

UNIT 4: Sew a Template D triangle and a reversed Template D triangle to either side of a Template C diamond. Make four.

UNIT 5: Sew a Template E piece and a reversed Template E piece to either side of a C diamond. Make four.

UNIT 6: Sew a Unit 4 and a Unit 5 to either side of a Template B point, as shown. Make four.

FINISHED BLOCK: Set in the four Unit 6 pieces to Unit 3 to complete the block.

Unit 4: Make four

Unit 5: Make four

Unit 6: Make four

Complete block

18. White Nights

(13⅞" Block)

Jinny Beyer, Jinny Beyer Studio design, 2007

Six pattern pieces (two of them reversed) are needed for *White Nights.* If your Fabric 13 has a mirror image motif, cut the template for pieces B and F so that a mirror image motif is centered in the middle of the piece (use *mirror line* on templates as a guide). On all pieces cut from border print fabric, be sure that a line from the border print falls just within the seam line so that it will show in the completed block. Use the Jinny Beyer Perfect Piecer, as described on page 13, to mark the stopping points and pivot places for the points and the set-in seams.

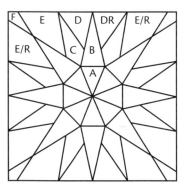

Template guide
(see page 78)

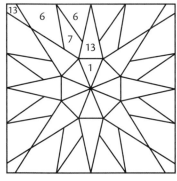

Fabric guide
(see chart on page 3)

Block Assembly

UNIT 1: Sew three Template A triangles together, then add a fourth triangle. Make two.

UNIT 2: Sew the two Unit 1 pieces together. Make one.

UNIT 3: Sew four Template B points to Unit 2, stopping sewing at the dots. Make one.

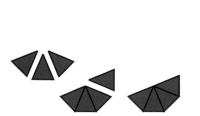

Unit 1: Make two

Unit 2: Make one

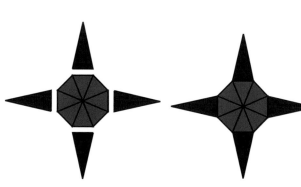

Unit 3: Make one

UNIT 4: Sew a Template D piece and a Template E piece to either side of a Template C piece. Make four.

UNIT 5: Sew a Template D reversed piece and a Template E reversed piece to either side of a Template C piece. Make four.

UNIT 6: Sew a Template F piece to Unit 4. Make four.

UNIT 7: Sew a Template B piece to Unit 5. Make four.

UNIT 8: Sew Unit 6 and Unit 7 together. Make four.

FINISHED BLOCK: Set in the four Unit 8 pieces to Unit 3 to complete the block.

Unit 4: Make four

Unit 5: Make four

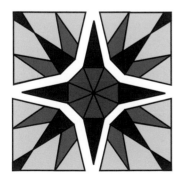

Unit 6: Make four

Unit 7: Make four

Unit 8: Make four

Complete block

19. Silver Star

(13⅞" Block)

Jinny Beyer, Jinny Beyer Studio design, 1999

Six pattern pieces (one of them reversed) are needed for *Silver Star*. Be sure to cut the border print fabric for the Template A and Template F (Fabric 1) pieces and the Template B mirror image fabric (Fabric 13) pieces, so that a mirror image motif is centered in the middle of the shapes (use *mirror line* on templates as a guide). Be sure that a line from the border print falls just within the seam line on pieces A and F so that it will show in the completed block. For Template E, the straight grain of the fabric should fall on the outside edge of the block (see template on page 79). Use the Jinny Beyer Perfect Piecer, as described on page 13, to mark the stopping points and pivot places for the points and the set-in seams.

Template guide
(see page 79)

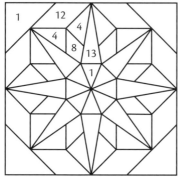

Fabric guide
(see chart on page 3)

Block Assembly

UNIT 1: Sew three Template A triangles together, then add a fourth triangle. Make two.

UNIT 2: Sew the two Unit 1 pieces together. Make one.

UNIT 3: Sew eight Template B points to Unit 2. Make one.

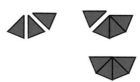

Unit 1: Make two

Unit 2: Make one

Unit 3: Make one

UNIT 4: Sew a Template D and a Template D reversed piece to either side of a Template C piece as shown. Make eight.

UNIT 5: Set in a Template E diamond, using the dots marked on the templates as guides. Make eight.

UNIT 6: Set the Unit 5 pieces into star Unit 3, pivoting at the dots. Make sure that the straight grain pieces of Template E fall on the outside edges of the block. Make one.

FINISHED BLOCK: Sew a Template F triangle to each corner of Unit 5 to complete the block.

Unit 4: Make eight

Unit 5: Make eight

Unit 6: Make one

Complete block

20. Cone Flower

(13⅞" Block)

Four pattern pieces are needed for *Cone Flower*. Be sure to cut the border print fabric for the Template B pieces so that a mirror image motif is centered in the middle of the piece (use *mirror line* on template as a guide), and so that a portion of the stripe shows at the base of the piece. All of these pieces should be identical. Use the Jinny Beyer Perfect Piecer, as described on page 13, to mark the stopping points and pivot places for the points and the set-in seams.

Jinny Beyer, Jinny Beyer Studio design, 1999

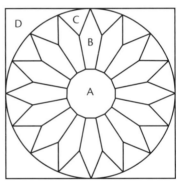

Template guide
(see page 80)

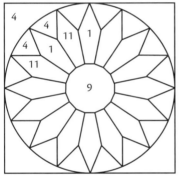

Fabric guide
(see chart on page 3)

Block Assembly

UNIT 1: Sew all 16 Template B points together, alternating fabrics as shown. Leave the last seam unstitched. Make one.

UNIT 2: Sew Unit 1 around the Template A center shape. Sew the last seam of the Template B points. Make one.

Unit 1: Make one

Unit 2: Make one

UNIT 3: Set the Template C wedges into Unit 2, pivoting at the dots marked on the B and C templates. Make one.

FINISHED BLOCK: Sew the four Unit 8 pieces onto Unit 3.

Unit 3: Make one

Complete block

Templates

Solid line = cutting line

Dashed line = sewing line

○ = pivot point for set-in seams (see page 15)

Mirror line = guide for cutting mirror images from border print fabric (see page 6)

Arrow = grain line (see page 4)

✁. Windmill

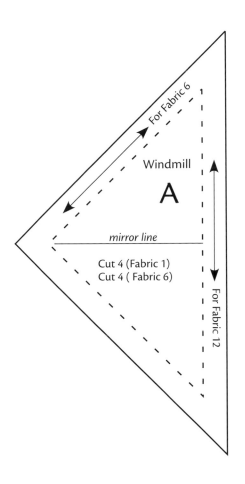

For Fabric 6

Windmill

A

mirror line

Cut 4 (Fabric 1)
Cut 4 (Fabric 6)

For Fabric 12

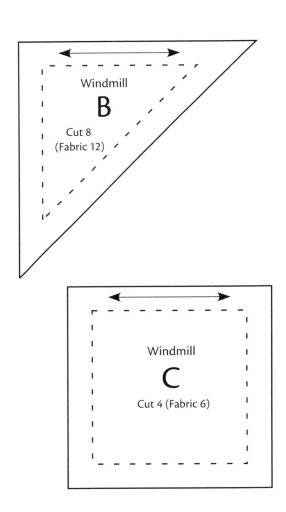

Windmill

B

Cut 8
(Fabric 12)

Windmill

C

Cut 4 (Fabric 6)

2. Mosaic No. 2

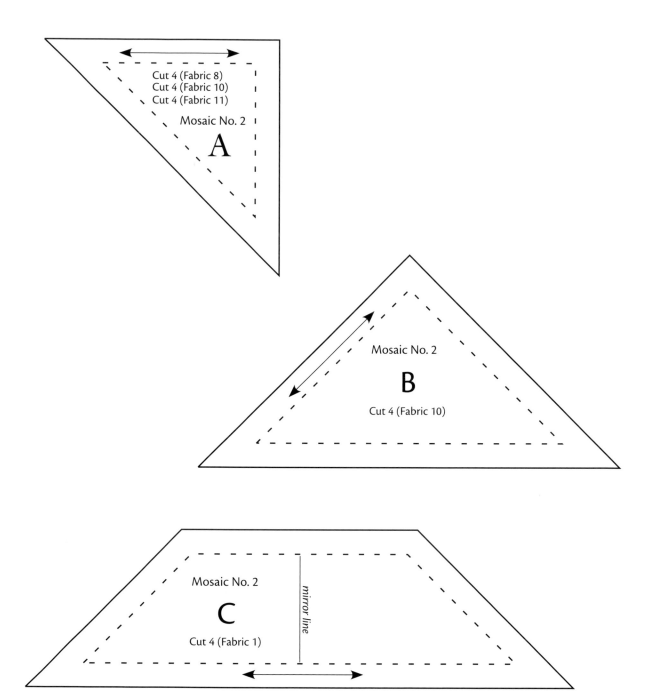

Cut 4 (Fabric 8)
Cut 4 (Fabric 10)
Cut 4 (Fabric 11)

Mosaic No. 2

A

Mosaic No. 2

B

Cut 4 (Fabric 10)

Mosaic No. 2

C

Cut 4 (Fabric 1)

mirror line

3. Double Wrench

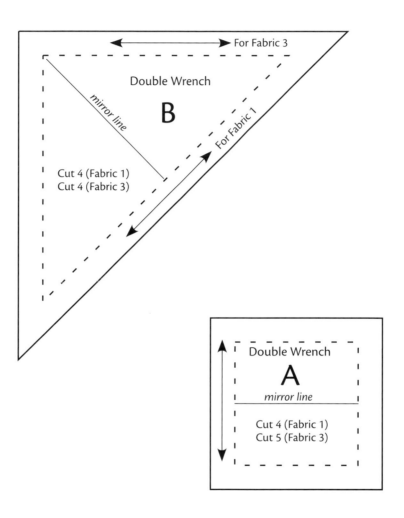

For Fabric 3

Double Wrench

B

mirror line

For Fabric 1

Cut 4 (Fabric 1)
Cut 4 (Fabric 3)

Double Wrench

A

mirror line

Cut 4 (Fabric 1)
Cut 5 (Fabric 3)

4. Sawtooth Patchwork

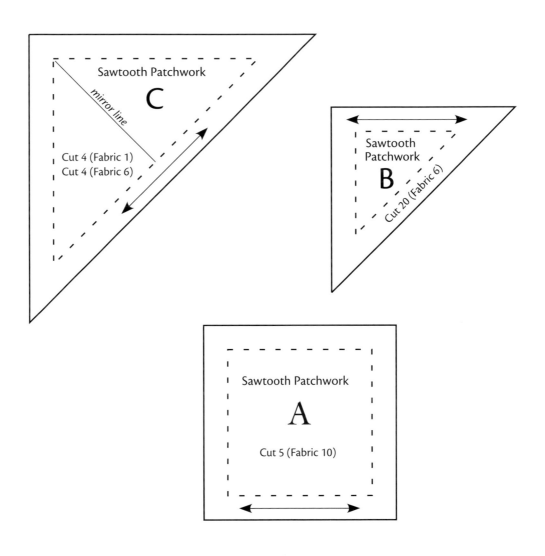

Sawtooth Patchwork

C

mirror line

Cut 4 (Fabric 1)
Cut 4 (Fabric 6)

Sawtooth
Patchwork

B

Cut 20 (Fabric 6)

Sawtooth Patchwork

A

Cut 5 (Fabric 10)

5. Card Trick

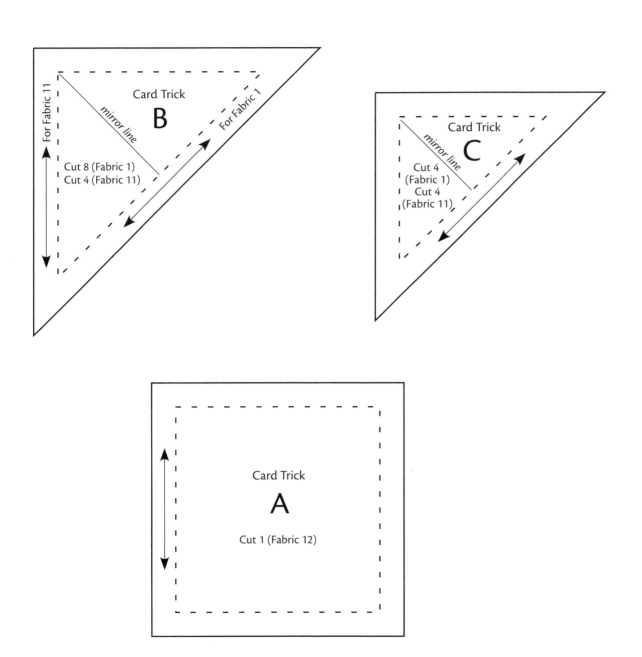

Card Trick

B

For Fabric 11

For Fabric 1

mirror line

Cut 8 (Fabric 1)
Cut 4 (Fabric 11)

Card Trick

C

mirror line

Cut 4
(Fabric 1)
Cut 4
(Fabric 11)

Card Trick

A

Cut 1 (Fabric 12)

6. Basket Quilt

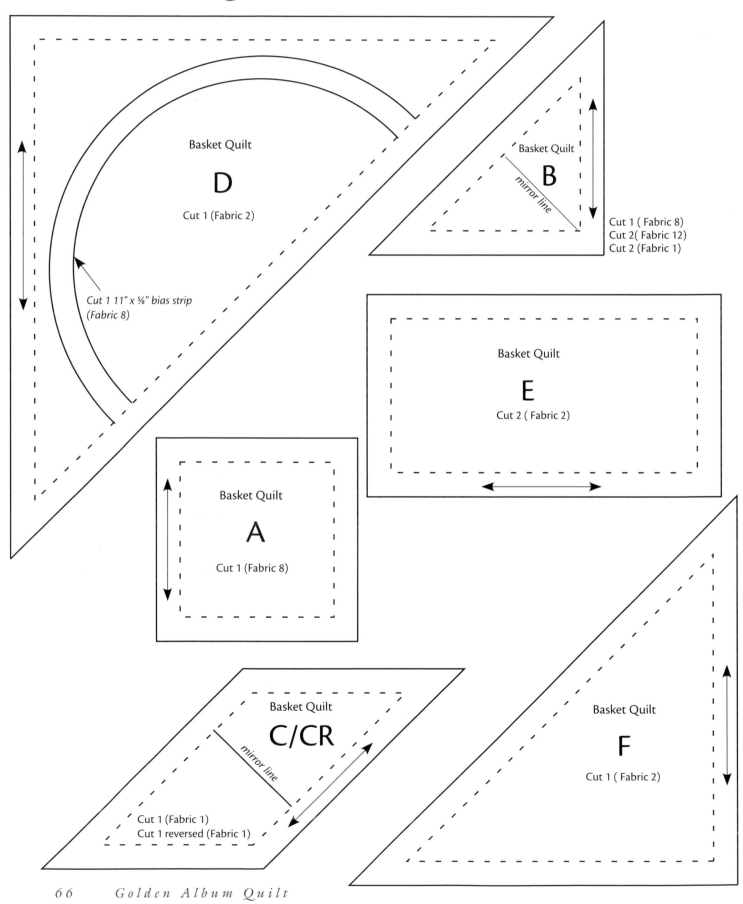

Basket Quilt

D

Cut 1 (Fabric 2)

Cut 1 11" x ⅝" bias strip (Fabric 8)

Basket Quilt

B

mirror line

Cut 1 (Fabric 8)
Cut 2(Fabric 12)
Cut 2 (Fabric 1)

Basket Quilt

E

Cut 2 (Fabric 2)

Basket Quilt

A

Cut 1 (Fabric 8)

Basket Quilt

C/CR

mirror line

Cut 1 (Fabric 1)
Cut 1 reversed (Fabric 1)

Basket Quilt

F

Cut 1 (Fabric 2)

✑ Johnny Around the Corner

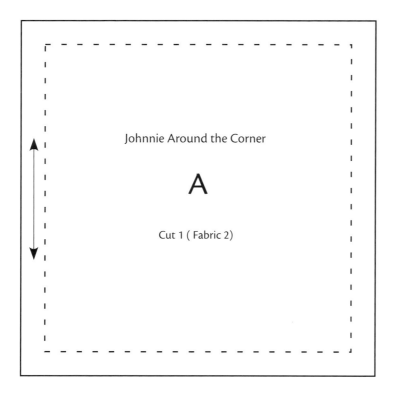

Johnnie Around the Corner

A

Cut 1 (Fabric 2)

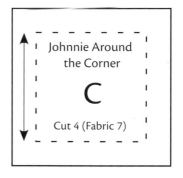

Johnnie Around the Corner

C

Cut 4 (Fabric 7)

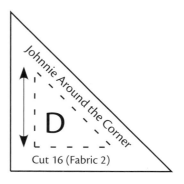

Johnnie Around the Corner

D

Cut 16 (Fabric 2)

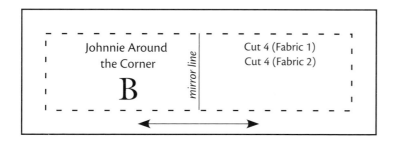

Johnnie Around the Corner

B

mirror line

Cut 4 (Fabric 1)
Cut 4 (Fabric 2)

8. The House That Jack Built

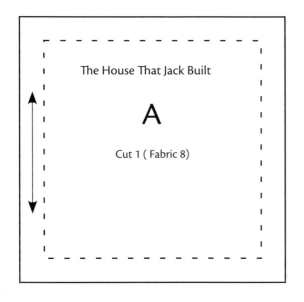

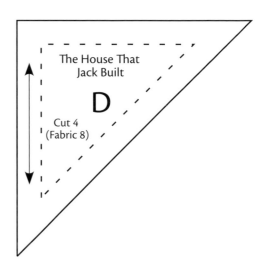

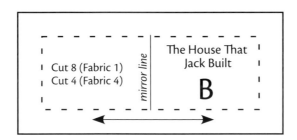

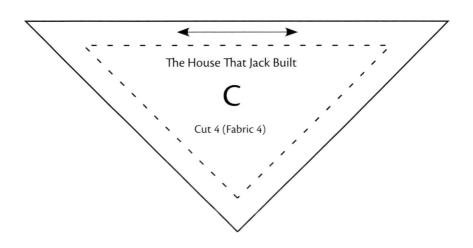

9. Lost Ship Pattern

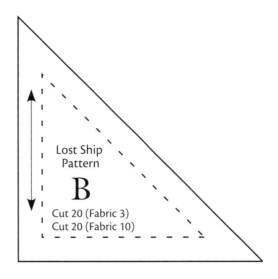

Lost Ship
Pattern

B

Cut 20 (Fabric 3)
Cut 20 (Fabric 10)

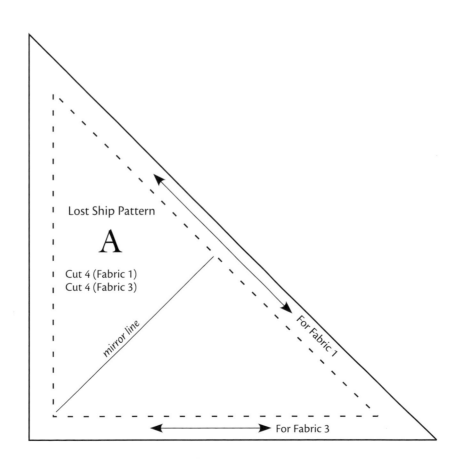

Lost Ship Pattern

A

Cut 4 (Fabric 1)
Cut 4 (Fabric 3)

mirror line

For Fabric 1

For Fabric 3

10. Lily Quilt Pattern

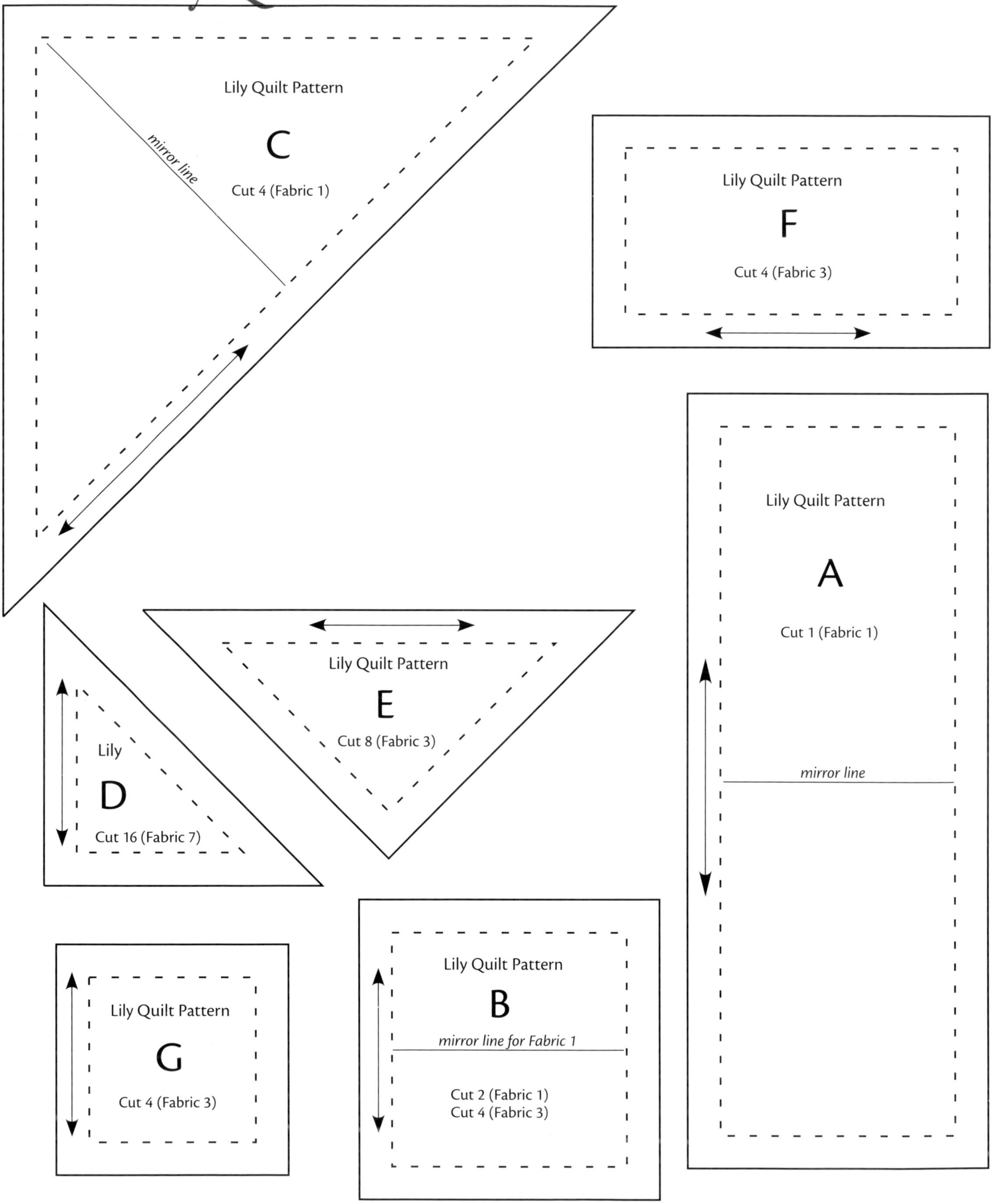

Lily Quilt Pattern

C

Cut 4 (Fabric 1)

mirror line

Lily Quilt Pattern

F

Cut 4 (Fabric 3)

Lily Quilt Pattern

A

Cut 1 (Fabric 1)

mirror line

Lily

D

Cut 16 (Fabric 7)

Lily Quilt Pattern

E

Cut 8 (Fabric 3)

Lily Quilt Pattern

G

Cut 4 (Fabric 3)

Lily Quilt Pattern

B

mirror line for Fabric 1

Cut 2 (Fabric 1)
Cut 4 (Fabric 3)

11. Burnham Square

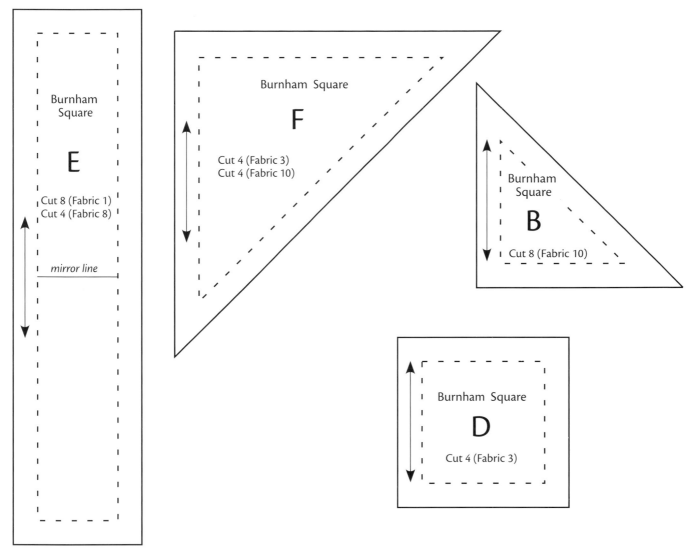

Burnham Square

E

Cut 8 (Fabric 1)
Cut 4 (Fabric 8)

mirror line

Burnham Square

F

Cut 4 (Fabric 3)
Cut 4 (Fabric 10)

Burnham
Square

B

Cut 8 (Fabric 10)

Burnham Square

D

Cut 4 (Fabric 3)

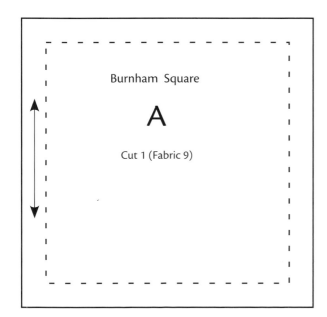

Burnham Square

A

Cut 1 (Fabric 9)

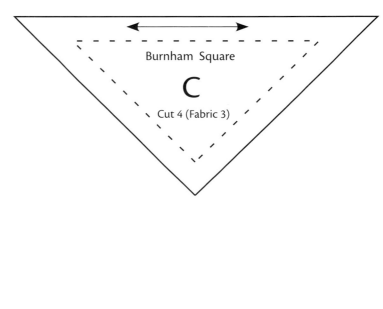

Burnham Square

C

Cut 4 (Fabric 3)

12. The Prosperity Block

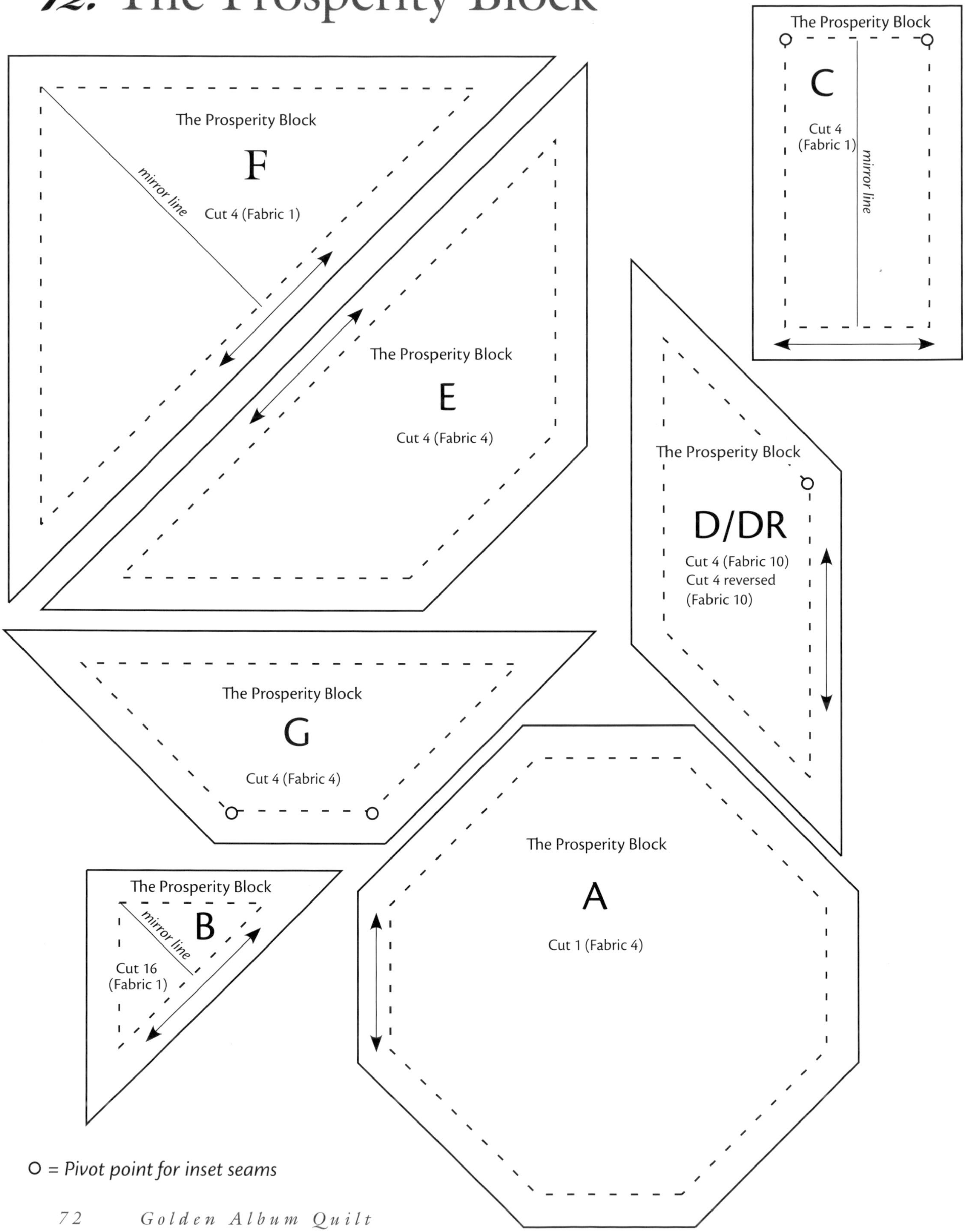

The Prosperity Block

F

mirror line

Cut 4 (Fabric 1)

The Prosperity Block

E

Cut 4 (Fabric 4)

The Prosperity Block

C

Cut 4
(Fabric 1)

mirror line

The Prosperity Block

D/DR

Cut 4 (Fabric 10)
Cut 4 reversed
(Fabric 10)

The Prosperity Block

G

Cut 4 (Fabric 4)

The Prosperity Block

A

Cut 1 (Fabric 4)

The Prosperity Block

B

mirror line

Cut 16
(Fabric 1)

○ = *Pivot point for inset seams*

13. Cross and Crown

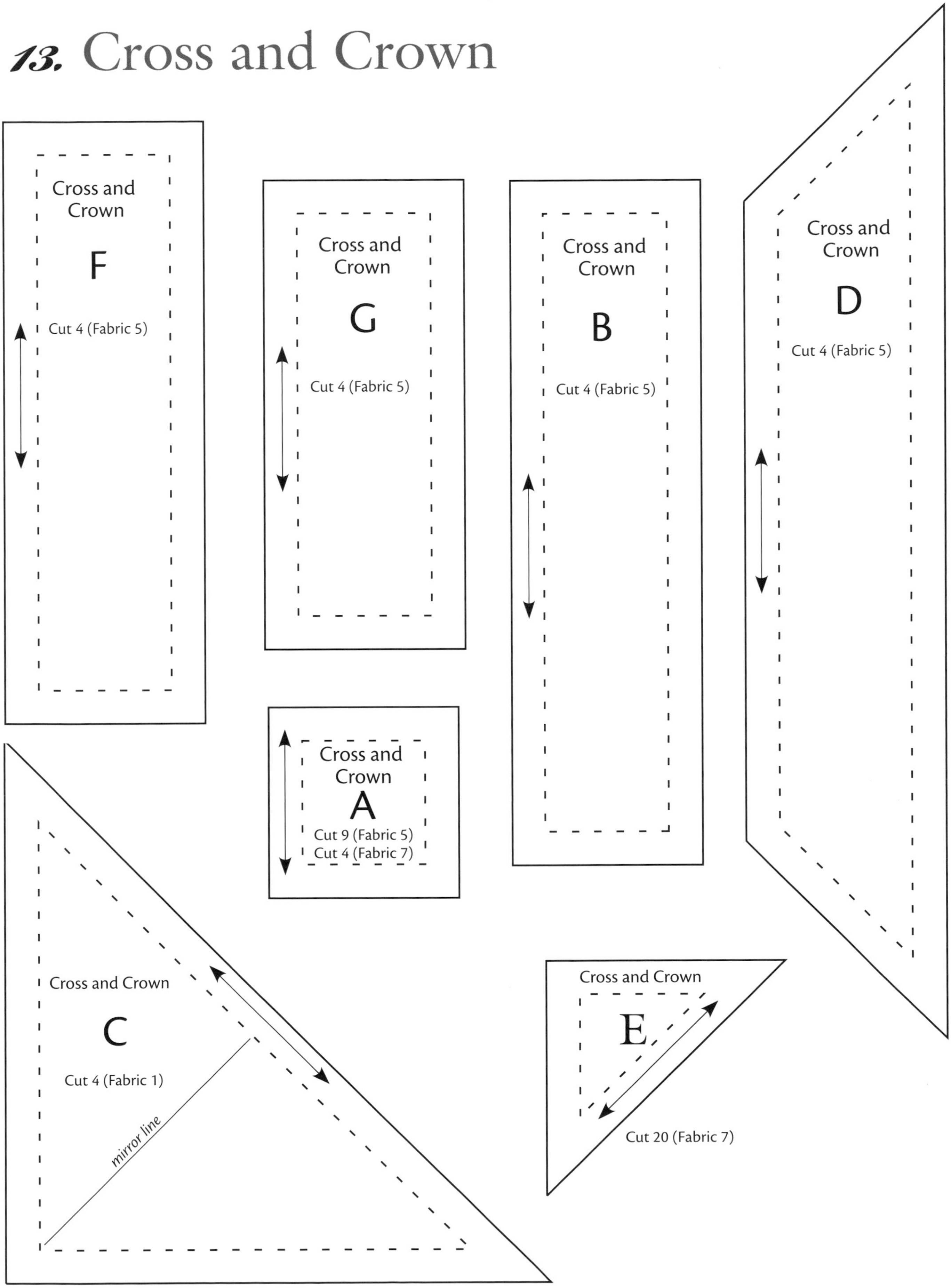

Cross and Crown

F

Cut 4 (Fabric 5)

Cross and Crown

G

Cut 4 (Fabric 5)

Cross and Crown

B

Cut 4 (Fabric 5)

Cross and Crown

D

Cut 4 (Fabric 5)

Cross and Crown

A

Cut 9 (Fabric 5)
Cut 4 (Fabric 7)

Cross and Crown

C

Cut 4 (Fabric 1)

mirror line

Cross and Crown

E

Cut 20 (Fabric 7)

14. Imperial T

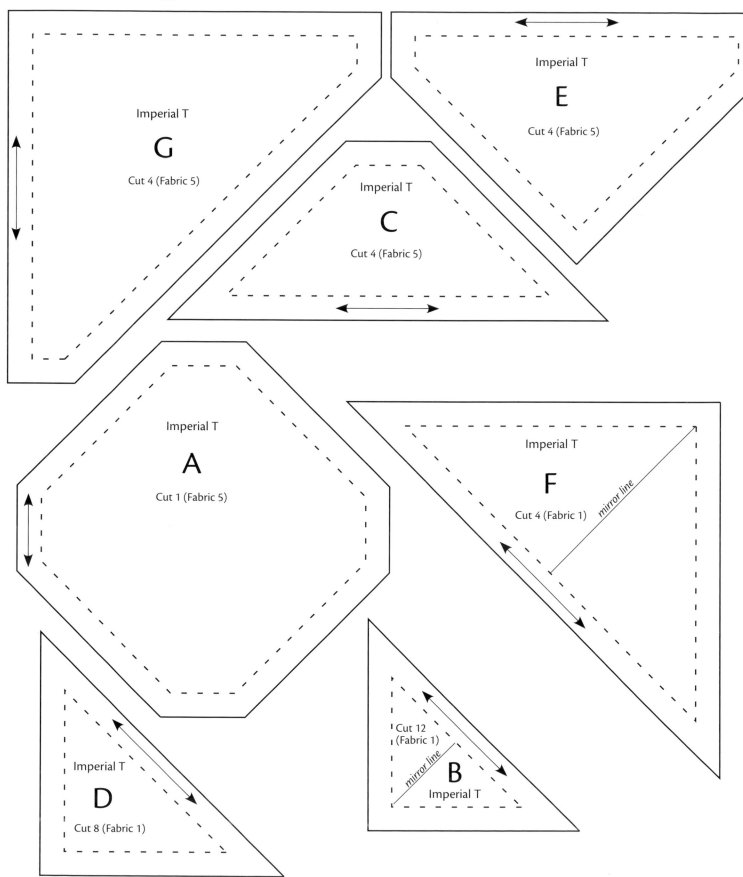

Imperial T

G

Cut 4 (Fabric 5)

Imperial T

E

Cut 4 (Fabric 5)

Imperial T

C

Cut 4 (Fabric 5)

Imperial T

A

Cut 1 (Fabric 5)

Imperial T

F

Cut 4 (Fabric 1)

mirror line

Imperial T

D

Cut 8 (Fabric 1)

Cut 12
(Fabric 1)

mirror line

B

Imperial T

15. The Royal

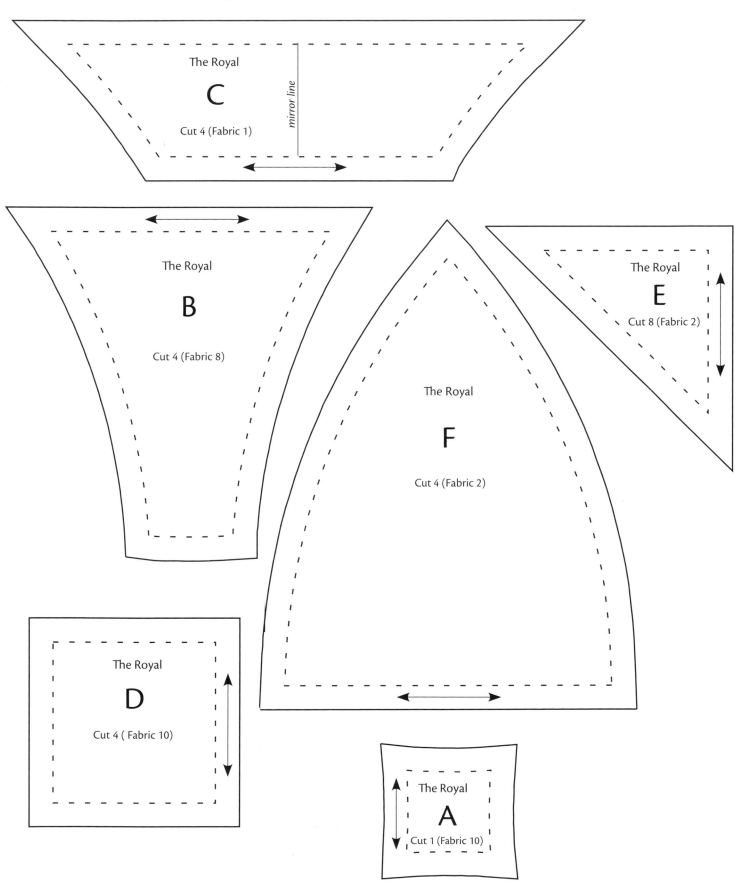

The Royal

C

Cut 4 (Fabric 1)

mirror line

The Royal

B

Cut 4 (Fabric 8)

The Royal

E

Cut 8 (Fabric 2)

The Royal

F

Cut 4 (Fabric 2)

The Royal

D

Cut 4 (Fabric 10)

The Royal

A

Cut 1 (Fabric 10)

16. Arrant Red Birds

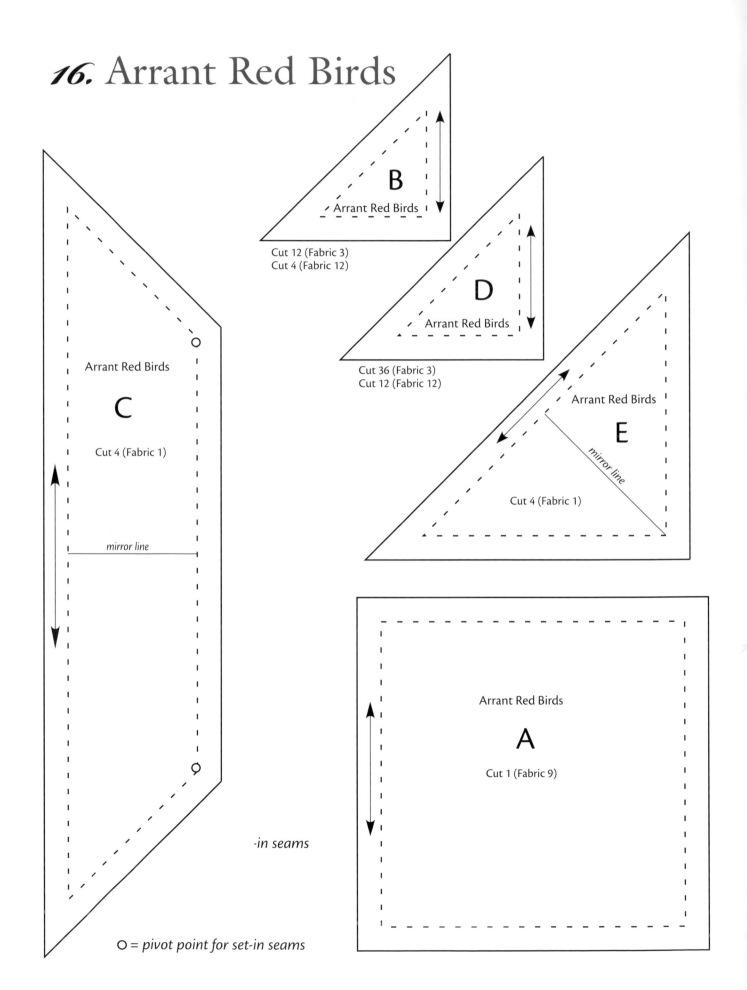

B

Arrant Red Birds

Cut 12 (Fabric 3)
Cut 4 (Fabric 12)

D

Arrant Red Birds

Cut 36 (Fabric 3)
Cut 12 (Fabric 12)

Arrant Red Birds

C

Cut 4 (Fabric 1)

mirror line

Arrant Red Birds

E

mirror line

Cut 4 (Fabric 1)

Arrant Red Birds

A

Cut 1 (Fabric 9)

-in seams

○ = *pivot point for set-in seams*

17. New Millenium

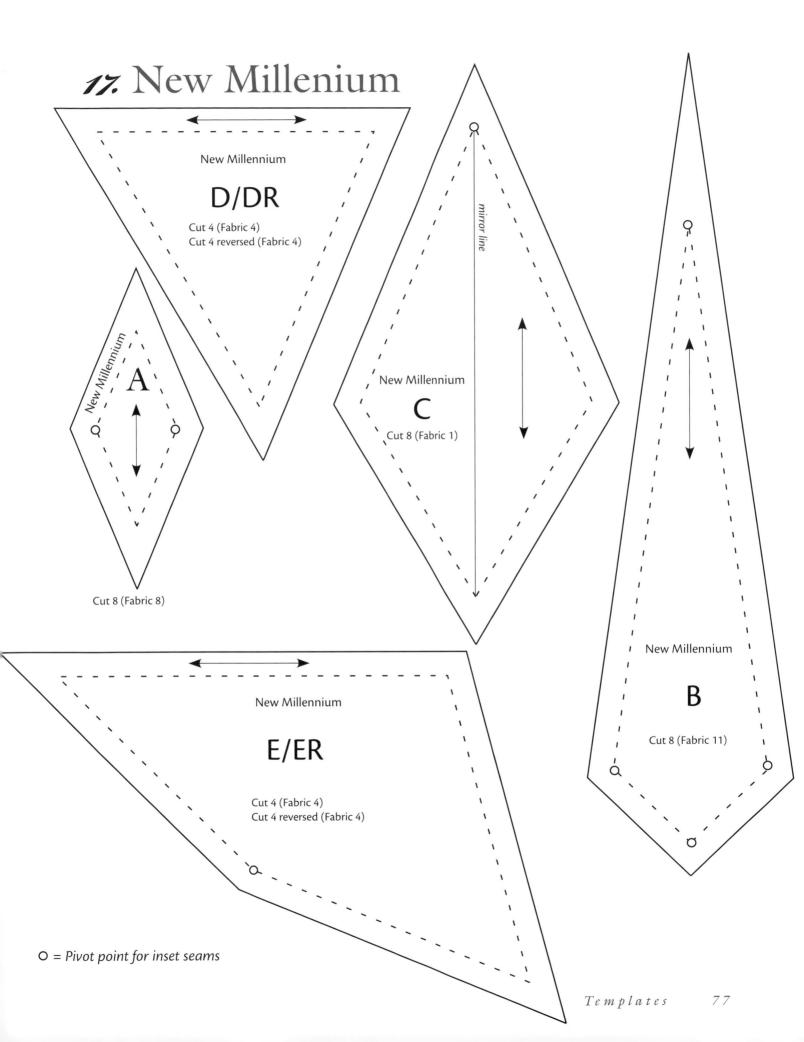

New Millennium

D/DR

Cut 4 (Fabric 4)
Cut 4 reversed (Fabric 4)

New Millennium

A

Cut 8 (Fabric 8)

New Millennium

C

Cut 8 (Fabric 1)

mirror line

New Millennium

B

Cut 8 (Fabric 11)

New Millennium

E/ER

Cut 4 (Fabric 4)
Cut 4 reversed (Fabric 4)

○ = *Pivot point for inset seams*

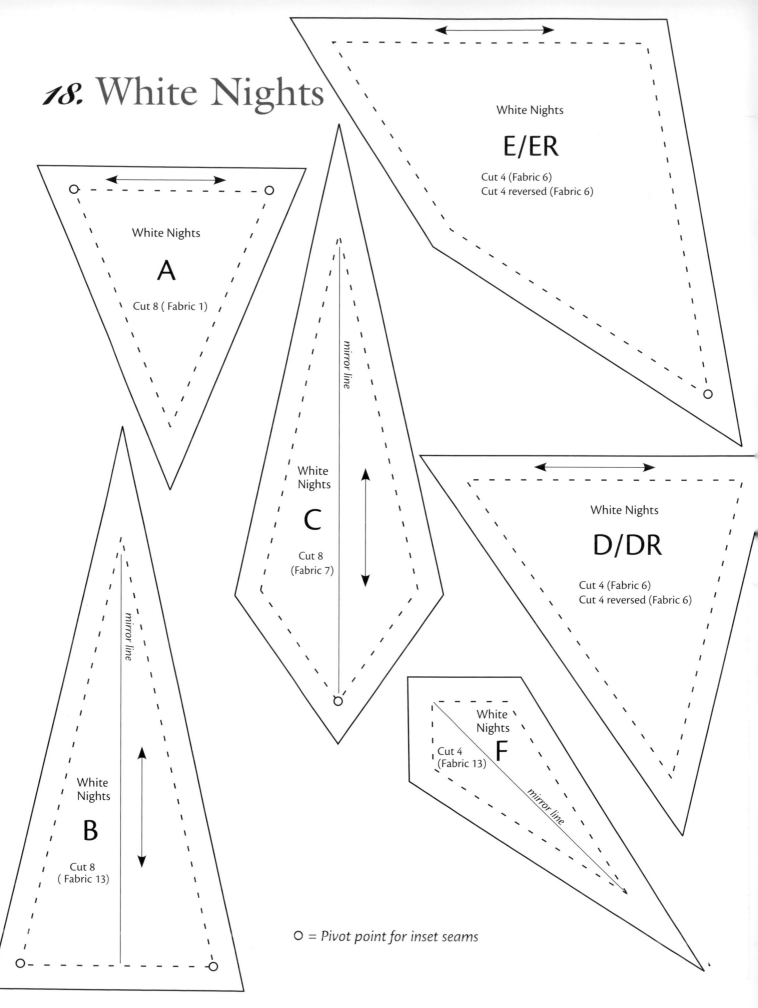

18. White Nights

White Nights

E/ER

Cut 4 (Fabric 6)
Cut 4 reversed (Fabric 6)

White Nights

A

Cut 8 (Fabric 1)

mirror line

White Nights

C

Cut 8
(Fabric 7)

White Nights

D/DR

Cut 4 (Fabric 6)
Cut 4 reversed (Fabric 6)

mirror line

White Nights

B

Cut 8
(Fabric 13)

White Nights

Cut 4
(Fabric 13)

F

mirror line

O = *Pivot point for inset seams*

19. Silver Star

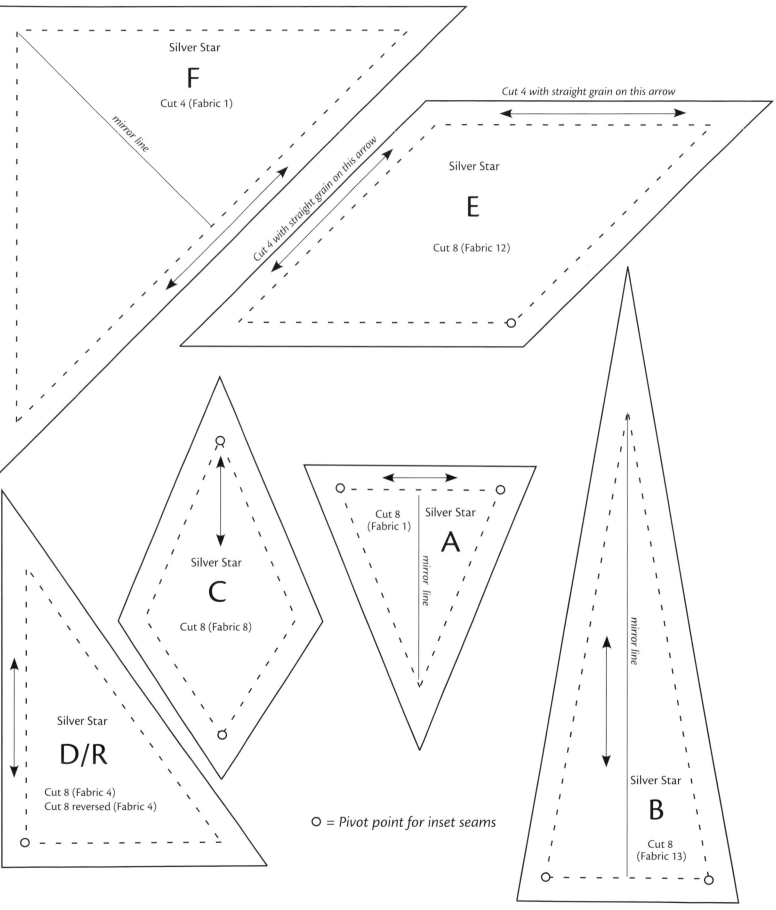

Silver Star

F

Cut 4 (Fabric 1)

mirror line

Cut 4 with straight grain on this arrow

Cut 4 with straight grain on this arrow

Silver Star

E

Cut 8 (Fabric 12)

Silver Star

C

Cut 8 (Fabric 8)

Cut 8
(Fabric 1)

Silver Star

A

mirror line

mirror line

Silver Star

D/R

Cut 8 (Fabric 4)
Cut 8 reversed (Fabric 4)

○ = *Pivot point for inset seams*

mirror line

Silver Star

B

Cut 8
(Fabric 13)

20. Cone Flower

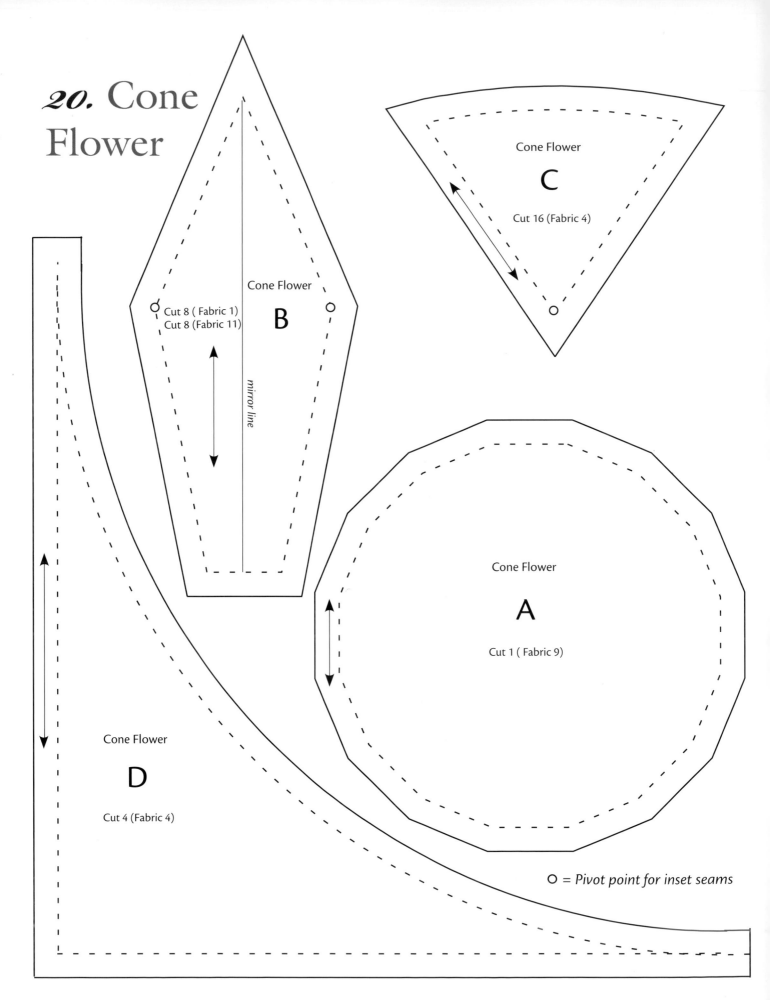

Cone Flower

C

Cut 16 (Fabric 4)

Cone Flower

B

Cut 8 (Fabric 1)
Cut 8 (Fabric 11)

mirror line

Cone Flower

A

Cut 1 (Fabric 9)

Cone Flower

D

Cut 4 (Fabric 4)

O = *Pivot point for inset seams*

Beyer, Jinny, *Quiltmaking by Hand*, Breckling Press, Elmhurst (Chicago), Illinois, 2004.

Beyer, Jinny, *The Quilter's Album of Patchwork Patterns*, Breckling Press, Elmhurst (Chicago), Illinois, 2009.

Country Gentleman, The, Curtis Publishing Company, Philadelphia, Pennsylvania. Vintage magazine established in 1890s. *Cross and Crown* was first published in *The Country Gentleman*

Chicago Tribune. Daily newspaper, Chicago, Illinois. Nancy Cabot was the pen name for Elizabeth Leitner Rising who wrote a quilt column for the newspaper from 1933 until early 1945. *Arrant Red Birds* was first published in *Chicago Tribune*.

Gutcheon, Beth, *The Perfect Patchwork Primer*, David McKay Co., Inc., New York, New York, 1973. *Card Trick* and *Johnnie Around the Corner* were first published in *The Perfect Patchwork Primer*.

Hilton Head Seminar designs. A series of patterns distributed at Jinny Beyer's annual Hilton Head Seminar, Hilton Head Island, South Carolina, from 1981 to 2009. *New Millenium* was first published as a Jinny Beyer Seminar design.

Jinny Beyer Studio designs. A series of quilt patterns produced by Jinny Beyer Studio, Great Falls, Virginia. *White Nights* and *Silver Star*, and *Cone Flower* are Jinny Beyer Studio designs.

Ladies Art Company. A pattern company established in 1889 in St. Louis, Missouri, that offered quilt patterns for sale through their catalogs from 1897 until the 1930s. Selections from *Ladies Art Company* are *Windmill, Mosaic No. 2, Double Wrench, Sawtooth Patchwork, Basket Quilt, The House That Jack Built, Lost Ship Pattern, Lily Quilt Pattern, Burnham Square, Imperial T,* and *The Royal*.

Quilt Booklet No.1, ed. Lois Schenk, *Prairie Farmer*, Chicago, Illinois, 1931. *Prairie Farmer* was a periodical published in Chicago which also sold mail-order patterns. *The Prosperity Block* was first published in *Quilt Booklet No. 1*.

Also Available from Breckling Press

The Quilter's Album of Patchwork Patterns This encyclopedia of quilt block designs provides quilters, researchers, and design enthusiasts with a comprehensive tool for finding, identifying, and drafting more than 4000 unique patterns. ISBN: 978-1-933308-08-1

Jinny Beyer Perfect Piecer This handy tool for machine or hand quilters saves time, increases accuracy, and helps piecers join six, eight, or more points with ease and speed. Order no: 0-9721-218-pp

Quiltmaking by Hand Richly illustrated and elegantly written, *Quiltmaking by Hand* showcases techniques for making quilts by hand. Jinny Beyer guides her readers through every step, from the basic running stitch to piecing perfect points to the final quilting. ISBN: 978-0-972121-82-8

Mystery Quilt Guide Designed to accompany *Quiltmaking by Hand*, this all-in-one teachers' resource provides everything a teacher needs to plan a six-week series of classes. Includes patterns for two original Jinny Beyer designs. ISBN: 978-0-972121-88-0

A Patchwork Notebook This keepsake journal lets quilters record their thoughts as they create a new quilt or sketch out designs. Includes gridded pages for drafting, inspiring quotes, and vintage engravings. Makes a perfect gift for quilters. ISBN: 978-0-972121-86-6

Hand Piecing with Jinny Beyer This all-in-one CD allows users to watch master quilter Jinny Beyer demonstrate hand piecing techniques and practice right alongside her. There are browser-accessed videos of precise hand movements for eight key techniques. Includes a pattern for an original Jinny Beyer design. PC/Mac compatible. ISBN: 978-1-933308-00-5

Patchwork Puzzle Balls Play with fabric in a fun new way! Jinny Beyer shows how to combine simple patchwork shapes to create perfectly round balls. Includes nine quick and simple designs, plus four more challenging puzzle balls. ISBN: 978-0-972121-85-9

Puzzle Ball Templates A set of five plastic templates to make quick work of cutting fabrics for the basic shapes required for making the first nine designs in *Patchwork Puzzle Balls*. Order no: 218-pp